THE TRADITIONAL
AGA
FOUR
SEASONS
COOKERY BOOK

THE TRADITIONAL

AGA FOUR SEASONS

COOKERY BOOK

Louise Walker

Absolute Press

First published in 2000 as
Louise Walker's
Four Seasons Aga Cookery Book.
This edition first published in
Great Britain in 2002 by Absolute Press
Reprinted September 2006

Absolute Press
Scarborough House
29 James Street West
Bath BA1 2BT
England
Phone 44 (0) 1225 316013
Fax 44 (0) 1225 445836
E-mail info@absolutepress.demon.co.uk
Website www.absolutepress.demon.co.uk

A catalogue record of this book is
available from the British Library

ISBN: 1899791248
ISBN 13: 9781899791248

Cover and text illustrations
by Caroline Nisbett

Printed and bound by Legoprint, Italy

Contents

GENERAL
INTRODUCTION

INTRODUCTION

Four seasons fill the measure of the year;
There are four seasons in the mind of men.
John Keates

As a nation many of us are becoming more aware of the food we eat: its origin, flavour and freshness. Do we really want or need to eat strawberries at Christmas and leeks from Australia in June? Surely we have enough variety on offer throughout the year, and usually with much more flavour. Of course, some foods that have become staples in our cookery have to be imported: where would we be without lemons? These, too, have a season and although we import them from around the world they certainly taste better when they are picked ripe in their correct season.

You may be lucky enough to grow your own fruit and vegetables and more and more people are returning to this rewarding occupation. Those of us who live in cities with only city gardens depend upon the markets and an ever expanding vegetable-box scheme. I have a weekly vegetable-box delivered to my door and each week it is fun to see what tasty organic vegetables it contains. Potatoes, onions and carrots are weekly staples and the rest depends on what is in season. In winter, there are more root vegetables, which are perfect for winter soups and casseroles. Spring brings the first baby carrots and new potatoes, the flavour so good that they are delicious on their own just with melted butter. Summer brings a variety of salad vegetables, and yes, they do need washing in salt water to kill the slugs and greenfly, but again the flavour makes the effort worthwhile. Autumn heralds the start of the mushroom season. Apples, pears and plums are at their best then and can be cooked in a variety of ways, perfect for the start of chilly days. (Most box scheme farmers offer other organic foods such as eggs, fruits and traditionally cured ham and bacon.) If you can't grow your own vegetables then I recommend this way of buying them. It will keep you in step with the seasons, offer you a variety of produce not always available in supermarkets and above all, the freshness and flavour are worth savouring.

Where I live in Bath, we have one of the very first farmers' markets, now held fortnightly. The stallholders must produce their wares themselves. At our market, foods available range from local organic vegetables, local cheeses, meats of all varieties, cakes, preserves, fruit juices, milk and cream. Doing a weekend shop there supports local producers and the produce is cheaper and fresher than in the nearby supermarket. Similar farmers' markets are opening all round the country, so look out for one near you.

The cry for more awareness of seasonal food is not new. I have been lent some fascinating old Aga books by the Aga cook, Irene Dunn. Back in 1933 Ambrose Heath wrote Good Food on the Aga, followed in 1937 by the Country Life Cookery Book in which he comments,

> *'I am not a believer in foods out of season, and I can never understand why so-called gourmets take the trouble to pay twenty-five or thirty shillings a pound for forced strawberries that have little or no flavour.'*

It would seem that food writers don't change!
No seasonal book is going to divide evenly. The seasons are dependant on the weather and we all know how the British weather can play tricks on us, so this book can only be a guideline, a sample of recipes and ideas, but once you start hunting for seasonal foods in markets and hedgerows your food is bound to become more varied. To quote Mr Ambrose Heath again,

> *'Food that is worth eating cannot usually be flung together and dished up in a hurry and I have assumed that those who will like and use this book will be those who are ready to give some thought and care to the preparation of their meals.'*

CONVERSION CHART

This is the metric/imperial chart that I abide by. Do keep to either metric or imperial measures throughout the whole recipe. Mixing the two can lead to all kinds of problems. Eggs used in testing have been size 3. "Tablespoon" and "teaspoon" measures have been flat unless otherwise stated.

Ingredients	Conversion
1 oz	25g
2 oz	50g
3 oz	75g
4 oz	100g
5 oz	150g
6 oz	175g
7 oz	200g
8 oz	225g
9 oz	250g
10 oz	275g
11 oz	300g
12 oz	350g
13 oz	375g
14 oz	400g
15 oz	425g
16 oz (1 lb)	450g
2 lb	1kg
1 tsp	5ml
1 tbsp	15ml
¼ pint	150ml
½ pint	300ml
¾ pint	450ml
1 pint	600ml
2 pints	1.2l
8-inch tin	20-cm tin

LOOKING AFTER YOUR AGA

Over the last few years Aga-Rayburn have brought out a few new items of cookware. I am lucky in that I can try these in the show-rooms during cookery demonstrations before I buy. Utensils are expensive and so you need to know that you will get value for money. All the Aga Shops and dealer's shops should have a good range of equipment. All the items made for Aga have been tested and, if looked after, will last as long as your Aga. I have seen a set of saucepans bought with a new Aga 48 years ago and just one handle had come off in that time! Remember to dry everything well before putting away, but that is easy, wash and put straight back on the Aga to dry. Don't put aluminium trays and pans in the dishwasher, the salt will eat them!

A new Aga comes with:

A large and small roasting tin with a grill rack inside each. These tins fit on the runners.

A cold shelf (plain shelf) to vary the oven temperature. Keep out of the oven so that it can be effective when you need it. It is also a useful baking tray for making giant pizzas.

Oven shelves. These are always the subject of 'help me out' at new owner demonstrations. The shelves have an anti-tilt design which is easy to use when you know what you are doing. However if you get your shelf stuck ask your service engineer or go to an Aga Shop where you can probably prac-tice on a cold Aga. Just remember, lift the shelf up before pulling out!

Although these are the basics that the Aga comes with, in my opinion there are three more essentials that I think new own-ers should buy:

An Aga kettle. What a waste of heat it is not to use a kettle on the Aga. Do remember to give it a rinse out at least once a day and keep it as scale-free as possible. Where I live, in Bath, we must have some of the hardest water in the country, keeping the spout of the kettle clean is a constant battle! If your kettle seems to take a long time to come to the boil give the hot plate a brush with the wire brush, just a few toast crumbs can stop the water boiling.

Gauntlets can take a little time to get used to but if you don't want burn marks up your arm they are an essential item. The Aga gauntlets can seem stiff and unwieldy when they are new but after a couple of washes they will soften up.

Bake-O-Glide is a great boon if you don't like washing up or cutting parchment to line cake tins. Bake-O-Glide is a reusable non-stick liner that simply needs a wash in hot soapy water after each use and will mean that tins only need a quick wash rather than a soak and scrub. This magic liner can be bought in a roll or, even easier, from the Aga shops you can get it as a set for all the Aga tins.

Apart from those essentials I have mentioned one or two other pieces of equipment throughout this book:

Baking tray. Several years ago Aga brought out a baking tray similar to the roasting tin. At first I couldn't see the reason to have a shallow tin when the roasting tin worked so well. Now I have to eat my words. I have the large and small size and use them practically every day. Because they are shallow roast vegetables, for example, cook faster and better than in the roasting tin. These tins of course fit on the oven runners. In some recipes in this book I have stated a shelf position. If you have the Aga tins use that runner or put the shelf on the runner suggested and your own tin on that.

The wok and the ridged pan. Aga now make a heavy wok with a flat base to make contact with the hotplate. To have a successful stir-fry it is essential that the wok is hot before you start cooking. Place the empty wok on the boiling plate for at least ten minutes, yes, ten minutes! During Aga demonstrations I know that the wok is getting hot because the audience shows signs of concern, expecting the whole thing to explode! When the wok is hot start cooking quickly as the oil will burn if you haven't got the ingredients ready to go in straight away. Similarly, the ridged pan. Choose one with deep ridges that can be heated well. Cast iron is the best, but heavy. There is never any need to put oil in these pans, anyway the oil would disappear into the base of the pan and be of no use. If you want to 'grill' vegetables, however, then brush them with oil before putting them in the pan. Again, you need to heat the pan for a minimum of ten minutes, and you can do this on the floor of the roasting oven if the pan handle is ovenproof.

A timer. This is essential as food cooking in the Aga will not be smelt, unless of course if you go in the garden! Try and obey the timer. I have two problems with timers. Firstly if I am busy when the timer rings I think I will check the ovens in a minute, and often don't! Secondly the timer rings and I can't think of anything in the oven so don't check! We have our fair share of charcoal dishes.

COOKING WITH THE AGA

You will have more success with your Aga if you understand the reasoning behind strange instructions like 'cooking potatoes in the oven'. The Aga uses stored heat. The ovens cook well when they are heated to their optimum temperature, your engineer will explain this, and will cook with a lovely even heat. As soon as the hotplate lids are lifted there is going to be some heat loss. Obviously this is not significant if just boiling a kettle or making toast, but cooking a pan of potatoes ready to mash will lower the oven temperature. So, always think, can this be done in the oven? The other advantage here is that you don't have pans boiling dry and steam and smells filling the kitchen.

To help keep the heat even in the Aga the lids on the hotplates are insulated and fairly heavy. Keep these lids down when not using the hotplates. The outer part of the lid is either chrome, stainless steel or cast iron. These will in time scratch so look after them. To non-Aga owners the boiling plate lid is the perfect place to put the kettle! Use a protective Chef's pad, folded tea towel or a trivet to protect the lids. I find that I don't use my hot plates very much. Boiling the kettle and making toast are the obvious examples. The boiling plate is also used to bring water to the boil, start vegetables or rice cooking, and of course wok cooking and making pancakes in a frying pan. The simmering plate is the place to make sauces, Welsh cakes and drop scones, toasted sandwiches and gravy.

Otherwise steaming, grilling and frying are usually done in the roasting oven. The ovens might look small from the outside but they are Tardis-like inside. The whole of the oven can be used as there is no single source of heat to spoil the food. It is not uncommon for the roasting oven to have an area where the food cooks marginally faster than the rest of the oven. All my gas Agas have been slightly hotter towards the back on the left-hand side of the roasting oven. This only causes a problem when doing large tray-bakes or trays of bread rolls, when turning the tray halfway through cooking usually solves that problem. All the ovens on an Aga, whether two or four are the same size. I once had a gentleman at a cookery demonstration who wished to see the room behind the Aga as he was con-vinced that I could not produce so much food from a two-oven Aga in the time. Needless to say he didn't manage to find the secret hatch to another cooker.

BASIC AGA TECHNIQUES

FISH

Cooking fish in the Aga is so easy and cuts out fishy smells. The variety of fish available is increasing all the time, so experiment with different fish and different cooking methods. I have given approximate cooking times, but this will depend upon the size and thickness of the fish. Try not to overcook as this gives dry, stringy, tasteless fish.

POACHING FISH

Place the fish in the roasting tin, cover with water, wine or milk, salt, pepper and a bayleaf. Cover it loosely with foil and hang the tin on the third set of runners from the top for 15-20 minutes.

POACHING WHOLE LARGE FISH (e.g. SALMON)

Clean the fish. Sprinkle with salt if desired and wrap in buttered foil. Lift the parcel into the large roasting tin, pour boiling water into the tin to come half-way up the fish. Hang on the second set of runners from the top of the roasting oven. Cook for 10 minutes per lb/450g, turning the fish half-way through cooking. Remove it from the oven and allow to cool. Serve warm or remove skin when cold.

FRIED FISH

Wash and dry the fish. If liked coat with either seasoned flour, batter, oatmeal or egg and fresh breadcrumbs. Put enough cooking oil into the roasting tin to coat the base. Put the tin on the floor of the roasting oven and heat until hazing. Add the fish and continue to cook on the floor of the oven. Turn the fish half-way through the cooking time.

GRILLED FISH

Lay fish cutlets in a roasting tin, brush with oil and seasoning. Hang the tin on the highest set of runners and grill, turning over half-way through the cooking time. You can ring the changes by marinading the fish for half an hour and grilling on the rack of the roasting tin, basting or brushing with a little more marinade part way through cooking. This will give a more charred appearance and taste.

MEAT

ROASTING MEAT

Meat roasted in the Aga will be moist and flavoursome with only a smearing of extra fat needed to start the cooking. Season as you prefer: salt, pepper, fresh herbs etc. If the meat is to be stuffed, do this and then weigh it to calculate cooking times. There are two methods of roasting using the Aga. The Quick Roasting Method is the more traditional method, used for more tender cuts of meat. The Slow Roasting Method is best for less fine cuts of meat.

QUICK-ROASTING METHOD

Season the meat and put in the Aga roasting tin. Stand it on the rack if you prefer. Hang the tin on the bottom set of runners of the roasting oven for the calculated time and baste periodically with hot fat. The shape of the joint will also affect the cooking time – a long narrow joint will not take so long as a short, fat joint. When the meat is cooked, allow the joint to rest in the simmering oven for 15 minutes before carving. This is a useful time to make gravy and cook last-minute vegetables.

SLOW-ROASTING METHOD

Season and prepare the meat as above. Put the roasting tin into the roasting oven on the bottom set of runners for 30 minutes or until the meat is browning and getting hot. Transfer to the bottom set of runners of the simmering oven and cook for twice the time calculated for the quick roasting method.

TIMES FOR ROASTING

Roast beef
(*rare*) 10 minutes per lb/450g, plus 10 minutes; or (*medium*) 15 minutes per lb/450g, plus 15 minutes; or (*well done*) 20 minutes per lb/450g, plus 20 minutes; (*fillet*) 10 minutes per lb/450g, plus 10 minutes

Roast pork
30 minutes per lb/450g, plus 30 minutes

Lamb
(*pink*) 15 minutes per lb/450g, plus 15 minutes; (*medium*) 20 minutes per lb/450g, plus 20 minutes

Veal
20 minutes per lb/450g, plus 20 minutes

ROASTING POULTRY AND GAME

Roast poultry and game from the Aga will be crisp-skinned on the outside with moist, tender flesh. Most poultry is cooked in the roasting oven by the normal method, but a large turkey can be cooked in the simmering oven, useful when cooking for a crowd or to take the rush and bustle from Christmas morning. Nowadays it is not considered safe to stuff poultry before roasting, though the neck end of turkey can still be filled if not the cavity. Always allow extra cooking time for this stuffing. Smear the bird with a little butter. Put bacon rashers over the breast if required and stand it on the trivet in the roasting tin. Put lemon or herbs in the body cavity if liked. Cover with a little foil – wrapping it tightly will slow the cooking time. Hang the tin on the lowest set of runners for the following times. Remove the foil for the last 1/4 hour to allow browning.

ROASTING TIMES

Chicken
45-50 minutes for 2lb/1kg; 1 hour for 3lb/1.5kg; 1 1/2 hours for 4lb/2kg; 1 3/4 hours for 5lb/2.5kg

Turkey
Weigh the bird after stuffing and allow 15 minutes per 450g/1lb, plus 15 minutes. Remove from oven and leave for 30 minutes to allow the flesh to firm up.

Duck
1-1½ hours

Goose
1½-2 hours

Grouse
30-35 minutes

Pigeon
20-35 minutes

Partridge
30-35 minutes

Pheasant
45-50 minutes

Quail
15 minutes

Snipe
15 minutes

Woodcock
15 minutes

Always ensure that the oven is up to the correct temperature before applying these roasting times. To test if cooked, pierce the thickest part of the thigh with a fine skewer, and if the juices run clear the bird is cooked. Allow the bird to rest in the simmering oven whilst making gravy from the skimmed cooking juices.

SLOW ROASTING OF TURKEY

Prepare the turkey in the usual way and stand it on the rack in the roasting tin. Cover loosely with foil and slide onto the floor of the simmering oven for the following length of time:

8-10lb/4-5kg: about 9-10 hours
11-15lb/5.5-7.5kg: about 11-12 hours
16-22lb/8-11kg: about 13-14 hours

Remove the foil and pop the turkey into the roasting oven for the last 15 minutes of cooking time to crisp the skin. Test in the usual way.

BOILED BACON AND GAMMON JOINTS

Cooking a whole piece of ham in the Aga is so easy and gives a moist joint, perfect for slicing. I even cook ham for friends because they love the moistness, and really it takes very little effort.

Soak the joint in water for 2-3 hours to remove any saltiness. Put a trivet or an old saucer in the bottom of a suitably sized pan. Put the joint on top and pour in enough cold water to come 2-3 inches up the side of the pan. Cover. Stand the pan on the simmering plate and bring slowly to the boil, simmering for 30 minutes. Transfer to the floor of the simmering oven for the following times:

2-3 lb/1-1.5kg: 2½ hours
4-5 lb/2-2.5kg: 3 hours
6-7 lb/3-3.5kg: 3½ hours
8-9 lb/4-4.5kg: 4½ hours
10-11 lb/5-5.5kg: 5½ hours
12-13 lb/6-6.5kg: 6½ hours
14-15 lb/7-7.5kg: 7½ hours
16 lb/7.5kg and over: overnight

Remove the pan from the oven and the ham from the pan and allow it to cool a little, to handle. Strip off the skin and score the fat. Mix together a glaze of mustard and honey and spread over the surface. Stud with cloves. Stand the ham in a roasting tin with the glazing uppermost and cover the meat with foil. Hang the tin so that the meat is fairly near the top of the roasting oven and bake for 10-20 minutes until a golden glaze has formed. Watch it closely, it may burn. Serve hot or cold.

STOCKS

Home-made stocks are easy to make in the Aga and they certainly taste better than stock cubes. If you make a large potful, freeze in quantities that are most useful: 1 pint/600ml for soups, ½ pint/300ml for gravies, etc.

BEEF, LAMB, CHICKEN, GAME, ETC.

Place the bones of the chosen meat in a large saucepan. Add a selection of flavouring vegetables e.g. onions, carrots, celery, washed and chopped, but not necessarily peeled. Add some peppercorns and a bouquet garni. Cover with cold water and put on a lid. Place on the boiling plate and bring to the boil. Transfer to the simmering plate and simmer for 10 minutes. Transfer to the simmering oven and leave for 12 hours or overnight. Remove the saucepan from the oven, cool and skim off excess fat. Strain through a sieve and either store in the fridge for immediate use, or freeze it. For a darker stock, roast the bones in a roasting tin on the bottom set of runners of the roasting oven for 45 minutes before proceeding as above.

VEGETABLE

Wash and chop a selection of vegetables, for example onions, carrots, leeks, celery, turnips, broccoli. Place them in a large pan and cover with water. Add a few peppercorns and a bouquet garni of whatever fresh herbs are to hand. Bring to the boil on the boiling plate, move to the simmering plate and simmer for 10 minutes. Transfer to the simmering oven and leave for 3-4 hours. Remove and strain through a sieve. Discard the now flavourless vegetables. Pack and freeze the cold stock or store in the fridge for immediate use.

FISH

Take a selection of bones from unsmoked fish and place in a saucepan. Add washed and roughly chopped vegetables like carrots and onions, a few peppercorns and a bouquet garni. Cover with fresh, cold water. Bring to the boil on the boiling plate, move to the simmering plate and simmer for 10 minutes. Transfer to the simmering oven and cook for 1 hour. Remove from the oven, strain through a sieve and store the cold stock in the fridge for 2 days or in the freezer for no more than 2 months.

BOILED POTATOES AND OTHER ROOT VEGETABLES

Potatoes, along with other root vegetables, are best cooked in the simmering oven. This both conserves the stored heat in the Aga and prevents the kitchen filling with steam. You will need to use a pan that can be used on the boiling plate and in the simmering oven, so avoid wooden handles. Do not be tempted to transfer the potatoes to a cold serving dish part of the way through cooking – the entire heat of the pan, water and vegetables is needed for successful cooking. Wash and prepare the potatoes in the usual way. Cut them to an even size. Place in the pan, add salt to taste, and cover with cold water. Put on the lid and bring to the boil on the boiling plate. When boiling well, pour off the water and transfer to the simmering oven. It is difficult to give timings, as the length of cooking time will depend upon the type of potato and the size of them. Allow 30 minutes and then test. Small new potatoes and small pieces of root vegetable will take about 20 minutes. Drain the vegetables, toss in butter if liked, and serve or return to the pan and the oven to keep warm.

ROASTING VEGETABLES

Roast vegetables are always a great favourite. I know that it is fashionably healthy to eat baked potatoes instead of roast, and steamed instead of roast parsnips, but nothing beats roast vegetables with roast meat for a special treat. Peel and cut the vegetables to an even size. Boil for one minute in salted water, then drain thoroughly. While the vegetables are draining and drying, put some cooking oil, lard or dripping into the roasting tin. Slide into the roasting oven on the second set of runners from the top. When the fat is hot, tip in the dry vegetables, toss them in the fat and return to the oven. If you are also roasting meat it may be necessary to juggle the tins during cooking. Cooking near the top will give an evenly cooked, crispy vegetable. Putting the tin on the floor of the oven will crisp the bottom of the vegetables well. They can be put into the top of the baking oven in the 4-oven Aga but they may need to be finally crisped in the top of the roasting oven. Vegetables take about 1 hour to roast. If the vegetables are put around the meat they may take longer and are often not so crispy, but they do taste wonderful!

COOKING RICE

A lot of people seem to have trouble cooking rice. Cooked in the simmering oven of the Aga, it is very simple, and it can be kept hot without spoiling if you want to cook it slightly in advance. This is the basic method for cooking rice. Adjust the quantities to suit your needs. Use a pan that will transfer from the boiling plate to the simmering oven.

1 cup rice
1¹/₂ cups water
good pinch salt

Wash the rice in a sieve with cold, running water and put it in the saucepan. Add salt and water and put on the lid. Bring to the boil on the boiling plate. When boiling, transfer the pan to the floor of the simmering oven. Cook for the appropriate time. The times I have given produce a cooked, non-soggy rice. If you like rice a little more cooked, then leave it in the oven a little longer. Remove from the oven and drain through a sieve – some rice will have absorbed all the water. Rinse with boiling water and serve. Alternatively, if you want to keep the rice hot, return it to the pan and stir in a small knob of butter. Cover and return to the simmering oven until required.

Cooking times:

White long-grain rice: 12 minutes
Brown long-grain rice: 20 minutes
Basmati rice: 12 minutes

Cooking Pasta

Pasta needs a fast boil when cooking, to prevent it sticking together. Try to use a pan that is deeper than its width. Half fill with water, add salt to taste, put the lid on and bring to the boil on the boiling plate. Add the pasta, fresh or dried, cover and bring back to the boil – this will not take long. Remove the lid and start timing according to the packet instructions. It may be necessary to move the pan half-on, half-off the boiling plate to prevent the water boiling over, but try to keep the water and pasta moving. When al dente, drain through a colander, return to the pan and toss in a little oil or butter to prevent sticking. Serve straight away with a chosen sauce.

Dried Beans and Peas

The range of dried beans available in the shops gives a whole host of flavours, colours and textures for cooking. The beans and other grains can be used for vegetarian cooking or to make meat dishes go further, or just to add variety. Lentils do not need soaking before cooking, just washing and picking over. All the other pulses need to be washed, picked over and left to soak for 8-12 hours or overnight, so some forethought is necessary.

Measure out the pulses required, wash well and pick over to remove any grit. Place in a bowl and cover with cold water. Put aside to soak. Drain the liquid from the beans. Place them in a saucepan, cover with cold water and bring to the boil. Boil rapidly for 10 minutes – to prevent the water from boiling over, use a large pan and no lid at this stage. After 10 minutes' rapid boil, cover and transfer to the simmering oven until tender, 1-3 hours. The length of time depends upon the type and age of the bean. Experience will be your best judge. When cooked, use as per recipe.

CAKES

During my Aga demonstrations I have heard so many people say, 'I am told you cannot make a cake in an Aga.' Nothing could be further from the truth, it is just a matter of knowing HOW to make a cake in an Aga. The 4-oven Aga has a special baking oven, so cake-making is easy. Just use that oven for all cakes, unless you wish to cook a rich fruit cake overnight in the simmering oven. The 2-oven Aga has a very hot roasting oven, which may seem too hot for cooking at lower temperatures.

Each Aga should have a large plain baking sheet, made of aluminium, known as the cold plain shelf. Cold is the most important word here. Store this shelf, not in the oven, but in a cool cupboard. The cold shelf is
put in above cakes or biscuits to reduce the top heat and allow the cake to cook through without burning. Always allow rising space and air circulation space – usually 2 runners above the oven shelf. If you are doing a large baking session, take the shelf out periodically to allow it to cool down and therefore become effective again. The cold plain shelf can be used as an oven shelf, and food such as scones can, of course, be put above it when it is being used as a cold shelf.

The other option for making deeper cakes that take several hours to bake is the Aga cake baker. The empty cake baker is heated up in the roasting oven while the cake is being made. The mixture is put into one of the tins provided, which is then put in the trivet and the whole thing put into the hot, empty cake baker. This is returned to the roasting oven and the cake cooked for the required time. The cake baker insulates the cake, allowing it to cook through without burning. If converting a recipe, check the cake during cooking as the final baking time may be shorter.

BREAD AND YEAST COOKERY

Bread and yeast-based dishes are so easy and successful using the Aga, not just because the roasting oven is so good for baking bread, but because the steady heat is perfect for warming and rising the bread dough. For a quick bread mix and for a store-cupboard stand-by, the easy-blend yeast in measured sachets is easy to use, and quick. However, if you have time, try using fresh yeast and let the dough rise twice, for a fuller flavour and better texture. Fresh yeast can be bought from health food shops, bakers and the fresh-bake counters in supermarkets. Store it in a plastic box in the fridge for about 10 days; should it go runny or smell rancid, throw it away and start with new yeast.

The choice of flour is largely personal. Organic flour comes in brown and white for bread-making, or standard strong white or brown can be used, or a mixture of both. Special flours such as rye or granary may be found at more specialist food shops. The quantities of liquids given in the recipes can only be guidelines, because all flours vary in the amount of liquid they absorb. Try to make the dough as moist as possible, without being too sticky to handle, as this will give a better finished product. The main problem with bread-making is trying not to kill the yeast. I warm the liquid by standing it on top of the Aga, so that it will be at blood heat and no hotter – it should be warm to the touch only. If the liquid is too hot, the yeast will be killed before it can do its work. I have given a few basic recipes, but once you have mastered the art of bread-making, you can enjoy trying out new ideas and new recipes from other books.

THE COUNTRY CALENDAR

 JANUARY

1st *New Year's Day*
5th *Twelfth night*
6-7th *pre-1752 Christmas Eve and Day.*
7th *St Distaff's Day.*
Housework begins after the festive holiday.
25th *Burns Night. Traditional ceremony of piping in the Haggis.*

 FEBRUARY

1st *End of pheasant and partridge seasons.*
14th *St Valentine's Day*

 MARCH

1st *St David's Day*
Collop Monday *All meat eaten in preparation for Lent.*
Shrove Tuesday *(Confession and shriving) Traditional time to use up all left-overs preceding Lent.*
Mothering Sunday

 APRIL

Carling Sunday *Pea dishes eaten*
Easter *(Named after the Saxon Goddess of Spring: Eostre)*
Good Friday *Hot cross buns*
Easter Day *Egg decorating and downhill rolling competitions. Simnel cake eaten.*

 MAY

May Day *First day of the Celtic Summer*
29th *Oak Apple Day celebrated by wearing an oak leaf in the lapel.*
Whitsun *Traditional holiday food includes Roast Veal and Gooseberry pudding.*
Whit Monday *Cheese rolling races in Gloucestershire.*

 JUNE

20th *Midsummer's eve. Bonfires lit to celebrate solstice.*
21st *Midsummer's day Sheep shearing commences, with shearing cake to eat and shearing ale to drink.*

JULY

1st Sunday *Gooseberry Pie Day*
15th *St Swithin's Day Blessing the*
  boats ceremony in Whitby, Lancashire.

 AUGUST

1st *Lammastide. Celebrate the first*
  harvest by eating a loaf made from the
  new wheat.
12th *Grouse season starts*

Throughout the month, summer fairs are
held on village greens.

 SEPTEMBER

Harvest Festival *Traditional ceremony*
  to celebrate the end of the harvest.
1st *Partridge season starts*
3rd *Nutting Day.*
  Children gather wild hazelnuts.
29th *Michaelmas Roast. 'Stubble' goose*
  eaten, goose fairs held around the
  country. Hiring fairs for new servants

 OCTOBER

1st *Pheasant season starts*
10th *Devil's Blackberry Day.*
  Last day for picking blackberries,
  after which the Devil is supposed
  to spit in the bushes making the
  berries poisonous.
31st *Hallowe'en. Carved pumpkins*
  to scare away evil spirits. In Scotland
  fortune-telling pudding' made.

 NOVEMBER

1st *All Saints Day*
  All Souls' Eve. Prayers said for the
  dead and food left on the kitchen
  tables during the night. Also, 'soulers'
  would go from door to door begging
  for soul-cakes.
5th *Guy Fawkes Day*

 DECEMBER

10th *End of grouse season*
21st *St Thomas' Day Traditional day*
  when the poor could beg for food.
24th *Christmas Eve*
25th *Christmas Day*
26th *Boxing Day*
31st *New Year's Eve*

BRITISH FRUIT & VEGETABLES IN SEASON

 ## JANUARY

Fruit *Apples (Cooking & Dessert), Pears* **Vegetables** *Jerusalem Artichokes, Beetroot, Brussels Sprouts, Cabbage, Carrots, Cauliflower, Celeriac, Chicory, Horseradish, Kale, Leeks, Lettuce, Mushrooms, Onions, Parsnips, Maincrop Potatoes, Turnips*

FEBRUARY

Fruit *Apples (Cooking & Dessert), Pears* **Vegetables** *Jerusalem Artichokes, Beetroot, Brussels Sprouts, Cabbage, Carrots, Cauliflower, Celeriac, Chicory, Horseradish, Kale, Leeks, Lettuce, Mushrooms, Parsnips, Maincrop Potatoes, Turnips*

 ## MARCH

Fruit *Apples (Cooking & Dessert), Pears, Rhubarb* **Vegetables** *Jerusalem Artichokes, Beetroot, Broccoli, Cabbage, Carrots, Cauliflower, Cucumbers, Horseradish, Kale, Leeks, Lettuce, Mushrooms, Parsnips, Potatoes, Swiss Chard, Watercress*

 ## APRIL

Fruit *Apples (Cooking & Dessert), Rhubarb* **Vegetables** *Jerusalem Artichokes, Beetroot, Broccoli, Brussels Sprouts, Cabbage, Carrots, Cauliflower, Celery, Cucumbers, Wild Garlic, Horseradish, Kale, Leeks, Lettuce, Mushrooms, Parsnips, Potatoes, Radishes, Swiss Chard, Watercress*

MAY

Fruit *Cooking Apples, Rhubarb, Strawberries* **Vegetables** *Asparagus, Beetroot, Broccoli, Carrots, Cauliflower, Celery, Cucumbers, Wild Garlic, Horseradish, Kale, Lettuce, Mushrooms, Peppers, Peas, Potatoes, Radishes, Swiss Chard, Watercress*

 ## JUNE

Fruit *Cooking Apples, Black-/Redcurrants, Cherries, Gooseberries, Plums, Raspberries, Rhubarb, Strawberries* **Vegetables** *Globe Artichokes, Asparagus, Broad Beans, Beetroot, Calabrese, Carrots, Cauliflower, Celery, Courgettes, Cucumbers, Endives, Fennel, Lettuce, Marrows, Mushrooms, Peppers, Peas, New Potatoes, Radishes*

JULY

Fruit *Black-/Redcurrants, Blueberries, Cherries, Gooseberries, Greengages, Loganberries, Mulberries, Plums, Raspberries, Strawberries* **Vegetables** *Globe Artichokes, Broad & Runner Beans, Beetroot, Calabrese, Carrots, Cauliflower, Celery, Courgettes, Cucumbers, Fennel, Lettuce, Marrows, Peppers, Peas, New Potatoes, Radishes*

 AUGUST

Fruit *Black-/Redcurrants, Blueberries, Cherries, Damsons, Gooseberries, Greengages, Loganberries, Mulberries, Pears, Plums, Raspberries, Strawberries* **Vegetables** *Globe Artichokes, Runner Beans, Beetroot, Calabrese, Carrots, Cauliflower, Celery, Courgettes, Cucumbers, Fennel, Leeks, Lettuce, Marrows, Peppers, Mushrooms, Peas, Potatoes, Pumpkin, Radishes, Tomatoes*

 SEPTEMBER

Fruit *Cooking Apples, Blackberries, Blueberries, Damsons, Raspberries, Pears, Plums, Strawberries* **Vegetables** *Globe Artichokes, Runner Beans, Beetroot, Calabrese, Cabbage, Carrots, Cauliflower, Celery, Courgettes, Cucumbers, Leeks, Lettuce, Marrows, Mushrooms, Onions, Parsnips, Peppers, Peas, Potatoes, Pumpkin, Radishes, Sweetcorn, Tomatoes*

 OCTOBER

Fruit *Apples (Cooking & Dessert), Blackberries, Chestnuts, Damsons, Hazelnuts, Medlars, Pears, Plums, Quinces, Strawberries* **Vegetables** *Jerusalem Artichokes, Runner Beans, Beetroot, Calabrese, Brussels Sprouts, Cabbage, Carrots, Cauliflower, Celery, Courgettes, Cucumbers, Leeks, Lettuce, Marrows, Mushrooms, Onions, Parsnips, Peppers, Peas, Potatoes, Pumpkin, Radishes*

 NOVEMBER

Fruit *Apples (Cooking & Dessert), Chestnuts, Medlars, Pears, Quinces* **Vegetables** *Jerusalem Artichokes, Beetroot, Brussels Sprouts, Cabbage, Carrots, Cauliflower, Celeriac, Celery, Kale, Leeks, Lettuce, Mushrooms, Onions, Parsnips, Potatoes, Turnips*

 DECEMBER

Fruit *Apples (Cooking & Dessert), Chestnuts, Pears* **Vegetables** *Jerusalem Artichokes, Beetroot, Brussels Sprouts, Cabbages, Carrots, Cauliflower, Celeriac, Celery, Chicory, Horseradish, Kale, Leeks, Lettuce, Mushrooms, Onions, Parsnips, Potatoes, Turnips*

SPRING

FRESH PEA SOUP

Pea soup looks fresh and appetising in spring, though it can easily be made at any time of year. Do not be tempted to leave the soup in the simmering oven for too long as the peas will lose their wonderful bright green colour.

25g/1oz butter
1 onion, finely chopped
150ml/$\frac{1}{4}$ pint white wine
1 litre/1$\frac{3}{4}$ pints vegetable or chicken stock
450g/1lb peas, shelled weight
150ml/$\frac{1}{4}$ pint single cream
salt & pepper
single cream and mint leaves, to serve

Melt the butter in a saucepan with a heatproof handle, or a flame-proof casserole, and fry the onion until soft but not brown. Add the wine and bring to the boil then add the stock and finally the peas. Cover, bring to the boil and transfer to the simmering oven for 20–30 minutes, until the peas are cooked.

Purée the mixture and then pass through a sieve. Return to the rinsed saucepan and stir in the cream. Warm through and check the seasoning.

Garnish with a swirl of cream and 1–2 mint leaves.

Serves 8

WATERCRESS SOUP

I love the fresh, peppery flavour of watercress. Sandwiches made of good fresh bread, butter and watercress are perfect. We are lucky enough to have good watercress in our weekly vegetable box during the spring months and it makes wonderful salads and sauces. It is equally good for soup.

25g/1oz butter
1 onion, chopped
2 potatoes, chopped
1 bunch of watercress
900ml/1½ pints vegetable stock
salt & pepper
150ml/¼ pint single cream

Melt the butter in a roomy saucepan with a heatproof handle, or a flameproof casserole, and fry the onions and potatoes until softening but not browning. Stir in the watercress and stock. Cover and bring to the boil and then move to the simmering oven for 30–40 minutes.

Remove the pan from the oven and purée the soup. Check the seasoning and return to the rinsed saucepan.

Heat through and swirl in the cream just before serving.

Serves 6

WILD GARLIC SOUP

In spring wild garlic grows in great profusion in the grounds of my daughter's school. The star shaped white flowers are so pretty, but the leaves give off a pungent smell when crushed. However, the leaves can be picked to make soup, and some people like them for salad, although I find them too tough unless they are very young.

1 tbsp olive oil
1 large onion, chopped
50g/2oz long-grain rice
225g/8oz wild garlic leaves, stalks removed & washed
225g/8oz spinach, stalks removed
900ml/1½ pints chicken or vegetable stock
salt & pepper

Heat the oil in a large saucepan with a heatproof handle, or a flame-proof casserole, and fry the onion until soft but not browned. Stir in the rice and toss well in the oil. Cook for 1–2 minutes before adding the wild garlic and the spinach leaves to the pan. Heat with the lid on for 1 minute while the leaves wilt. Add the stock and salt and pepper and bring to the boil. Cover and transfer to the simmering oven for about 20 minutes, until the rice is tender and the leaves are soft. Remove from the oven and purée.

Return to the rinsed pan, adjust the seasoning and re-heat. Serve immediately.

Serves 6

TOMATO CROSTINI WITH GOATS' CHEESE

Although goats' cheese is available all year round, if you use locally-made cheese you will find that those made from fresh milk in the spring and early summer have a particularly fresh taste. Experiment with different types of goats' cheese.

1/2 white French loaf, cut into 2cm/3/4 inch slices
6 ripe tomatoes, sliced
a few basil leaves
olive oil
1/2 soft goats' cheeses, depending upon the type chosen, sliced

Lay the bread on a baking tray. Slide into the top of the roasting oven and toast the bread.

Remove the bread from the oven and drizzle a little olive oil onto each slice. Divide the tomatoes among the pieces of bread. Tear the basil leaves and sprinkle over the tomatoes. Lay the goats' cheese on top.

Put the baking tray back onto the second set of runners of the roasting oven and grill for about 5 minutes, until the cheese is just turning golden and starting to bubble. Serve immediately.

Makes 8

GRILLED SALMON WITH ASPARAGUS SAUCE

May heralds the start of the English asparagus season, just as the time arrives for lighter meals. Fresh, young asparagus is so delicious I like it served simply with melted butter, but to make the most of the short season this is a lovely starter or main course. If you have a cast-iron ridged pan, use it to cook the salmon.

2 bunches of asparagus, about 40 stalks
25g/1oz butter
juice of ½ lemon
salt
pinch of sugar
250ml/9fl oz crème fraîche
pepper
4 slices of salmon fillet, skinned

If the asparagus stalks are a little woody, peel them lightly with a potato peeler. Bring a large pan of water to the boil and add the butter, lemon juice, a pinch of salt and sugar. Add the asparagus and cook until tender. Drain and trim off the tips of about 12 stalks to use as a garnish. Purée the remaining asparagus and then push through a sieve.

Mix the sieved asparagus with the crème fraîche and salt and pepper. Chill the sauce and just before cooking the salmon divide it among 4 serving plates.

Heat a ridged pan on the boiling plate for 5 minutes and then cook the salmon slices for 1–2 minutes on each side, depending upon the thickness of the fish. When just cooked through, place a salmon slice on each plate of sauce and garnish with the reserved asparagus tips.

Serves 4

PLAICE IN A POTATO CRUST

Plaice is most suitable when you feel like a light meal, usually in spring when you've had a surfeit of heavy and hearty winter meals.

4 cleaned whole plaice
2 potatoes, coarsely grated
salt & pepper
1 tbsp flour
1 egg white, lightly whisked
1/2 tsp thyme leaves
50g/2oz butter

Remove the heads and fins from the plaice and rinse the fish well. Dry thoroughly with kitchen paper. Dry the potatoes on kitchen paper too. Season the fish with salt and pepper and then dust with the flour. Dip the fish into the egg.

Mix the potato with the thyme and coat both sides of the fish with the potato, pressing on firmly. Place the butter in the small or large roasting tin, depending on the size of the fish, and put on the floor of the roasting oven until the butter is melted and hot. Lay in the fish and return to the floor of the oven to cook the plaice for 5 minutes on each side, until the potato is golden-brown and the fish is cooked.

Serves 4

SMOKED HADDOCK FLAN

Smoked haddock makes a tasty flan that is just right for serving with a salad and good home-baked bread in spring. Un-dyed fish has a better flavour than the dyed type but will be less attractive. I go for flavour.

225g/8oz shortcrust pastry
450g/1lb smoked haddock
150ml/¼ pint milk
pepper
150ml/¼ pint double cream
3 eggs, beaten
paprika

Roll the shortcrust pastry to fit a flan dish or tin 20–23cm (8–9 inches) in diameter. Chill.

Place the fish, skin side down, in a small roasting tin or an ovenproof dish. Pour on the milk and add a seasoning of pepper. Place in the middle of the roasting oven and poach for 15–20 minutes, until the fish is just forming into flakes in the thickest part of the fillet. Take care not to overcook the fish at this stage as it will be cooked for a second time in the pastry case. Lift the fish from the milk and reserve the milk.

Cool the fish slightly and then remove any skin and bones. Break the fish into large flakes and put in the base of the pastry case.

Beat together the strained poaching milk, the cream and eggs. Pour over the fish and sprinkle on a pinch of paprika. Bake on the floor of the roasting oven for 20–25 minutes, until the filling has set.

Serves 4

FISH PARCELS
WITH SPINACH SAUCE

For this recipe, choose a firm fish such as haddock or cod. Remove any skin and bone and make the fish into a reasonable shape to wrap into a parcel. Thin slivers of sautéd mushrooms or chopped fresh herbs can be added to each parcel, but do not use anything with too strong a flavour that will detract from the fish.

75g/3oz butter
225g/8oz fresh spinach
salt & pepper
grated nutmeg
8 small sheets of filo pastry
4 fish steaks, skin & bone removed

Place the butter in a small basin and stand at the back of the Aga to melt.

Place the wet spinach in a saucepan, cover with a lid and cook on the simmering plate until the spinach has wilted and is tender. Remove from the heat and purée. Season with salt, pepper and nutmeg. Return to the rinsed saucepan and set aside.

Butter 4 sheets of filo pastry and then cover each one with another sheet and brush with butter. Place a fish steak on top and season well. Wrap the pastry round to make neat parcels. Brush well with butter and place on a baking tray. Put the oven shelf on the second set of runners from the top of the roasting oven and slide in the fish parcels to bake for 20 minutes. The pastry should be crisp and golden-brown.

Pour any remaining butter into the spinach sauce and heat gently. Spoon some spinach onto each serving plate and lay a fish parcel on top. Serve immediately.

Serves 4

MARINATED MACKEREL

Prepare this dish the day before eating to let the flavours develop and the fish become really cold.

4 small mackerel fillets
4 bay leaves
2 tbsp demerara sugar
salt
6 black peppercorns
150ml/¹/₄ pint cider vinegar
150ml/¹/₄ pint cold black tea

Lay the mackerel in a shallow, ovenproof dish. Place a bay leaf on each fillet. Sprinkle over the sugar, a pinch of salt, and the peppercorns. Pour around the vinegar and tea. Cover with a lid or foil.

For a two-oven Aga, place the shelf on the floor of the roasting oven and put in the fish.

For a four-oven Aga, place the shelf on the second set of runners from the bottom of the baking oven and put in the fish.

Cook the fish for 15–20 minutes, until tender. Remove from the oven and allow to cool. Serve with bread.

Serves 4 as a starter, 2 as a main course

STEAK AND MUSHROOM PARCELS

Whole steaks wrapped in pastry make an easy way to serve steak that does not involve standing over a hot pan at the last minute. These parcels can be prepared several hours in advance and kept chilled until shortly before baking.

4 x 100g/4oz fillet or sirloin steaks
1 tbsp olive oil
1 small onion, finely chopped
50g/2oz button mushrooms, finely chopped
2 tbsp chopped parsley
1 tsp mustard
salt & pepper
225g/8oz shortcrust pastry
1 egg, beaten, to glaze

Heat a heavy frying pan until it is really hot, add the steaks and cook for 2–3 minutes on each side. Remove the steaks and then add the oil to the pan and cook the onion until softening but not browning. Stir in the mushrooms and cook for 4–5 minutes. Remove the pan from the heat and add the parsley, mustard and salt and pepper. Leave to cool.

Roll out the pastry to a large square and cut into 4 portions twice the size of each steak. Place a quarter of the mushroom mixture in the centre of each pastry square and then lay a steak on top. Brush the edges of the pastry with the egg and seal the pastry around the meat. Turn over and place on a baking tray so that the join is underneath. Brush the pastry with more beaten egg and use any pastry trimmings to decorate each parcel.

Bake on the second set of runners from the top of the roasting oven for 15–20 minutes, until the pastry is golden-brown. Then move the tray to the floor of the oven for 5 minutes to crisp the base.

Serve immediately.

Serves 4

GRILLED STEAKS
WITH HORSERADISH SAUCE

Serve this dish in spring, accompanied by boiled new potatoes and a bowl of tender young salad leaves. If you don't have fresh horseradish to grate, try and find a jar of grated horseradish.

1 tbsp grated horseradish
1 tsp lemon juice
mustard powder
salt & pepper
75ml/3fl oz double cream, whipped
4 rump or sirloin steaks

Fold the horseradish, lemon juice, pinch of mustard powder, and salt and pepper into the cream. Chill.

Heat a ridged pan on the boiling plate for at least 5 minutes, until really hot. Place the steaks in the searingly hot pan for 4–5 minutes on each side. Serve immediately with a spoonful of the horseradish sauce on the side of each steak.

Serves 4

LAMBURGERS
WITH GOATS' CHEESE

I make these burgers in the spring when the first of the fresh local goats' cheese becomes available and mint is in the garden. The burgers will shrink during cooking so make them larger than the baps.

1kg/2lb minced lamb
2 cloves of garlic, crushed
4 tbsp Worcestershire sauce
1 tbsp chopped mint
salt & pepper
225g/8oz soft goats' cheese, cut into eight slices
8 baps

Place the lamb, garlic, Worcestershire sauce, mint and salt and pepper into a mixing bowl and mix together really well. I find that this is best done using your hand. Taking a tablespoon of mixture at a time, shape into a burger and place on a baking tray. At this stage it is a good idea to chill the burgers for 1–2 hours, though it is not essential.

Hang the oven shelf on the second set of runners from the top of the roasting oven and slide in the tray of burgers. Cook for 10 minutes on each side. Place a burger on each bap and add a slice of goats cheese, which should melt slowly on top in the warmth of the burger.

Makes 8

ROAST LAMB ON RATATOUILLE

A simple way to prepare meat and vegetables in one pan. Roast some potatoes on the floor of the roasting oven beneath the lamb during the last hour of cooking. Vegetables cooked in this way are deliciously sweet.

2kg/4½ lb leg lamb
2 cloves of garlic, sliced
2 aubergines, sliced
1 onion, cut into 8 wedges
1 red pepper, seeded & cut into chunks
1 yellow pepper, seeded & cut into chunks
2 courgettes, sliced
4 tomatoes, quartered
2 tbsp olive oil
salt & pepper

Make several slits in the leg of lamb and insert slices of garlic. Stand the rack inside the roasting tin and put the lamb on top. Hang the tin on the third set of runners from the top of the roasting oven and roast the lamb for 25 minutes per 450g (1lb) plus 25 minutes.

One hour before the end of the roasting time, remove the lamb and rack from the tin and put the vegetables in the tin. Drizzle over the olive oil, season with salt and place the lamb, on the rack, back on top of the vegetables. Return to the oven for the remaining time. Remove the lamb and allow to 'rest' for 10 minutes before serving with the ratatouille.

Serves 6–8

SPICED LAMB WITH TOMATOES

This is a lamb dish for chilly spring days when the lightness of lamb seems right but the weather outside is far from spring-like.

1 tbsp vegetable oil
1kg/2lb neck of lamb chops
2 onions, chopped
3 cloves of garlic, crushed
1/2 teaspoon chilli powder
1 tsp sugar
2 x 400g/14oz can tomatoes
2 cinnamon sticks
salt & pepper

Heat the oil in a flameproof casserole and brown the chops on both sides. Add the onions, stir well and cook until softened. Then add the garlic and chilli powder and cook for 2 minutes. Stir in the sugar, tomatoes, cinnamon sticks and salt and pepper.

Cover and bring to the boil and then transfer to the simmering oven for 1½ –2 hours, until the meat is tender.

Serves 4

MINTED LAMB FILLET

Lamb fillet is tender and quick to cook, which of course makes it expensive, but there is no bone.

25g/1oz butter, softened
2 tbsp chopped mint
salt & pepper
1 lamb fillet, trimmed of excess fat

Mix the butter with the mint and salt and pepper.

Spread the minted butter over the lamb. Lay the fillet on a baking tray and place on the second set of runners from the top of the roasting oven for 10 minutes. Turn the fillet over and roast again for 10–15 minutes, depending on the thickness of the fillet. Remove from the oven and slice into portions about 2.5cm (1 inch) thick. Serve with new potatoes and young carrots.

Serves 2

PARSLEY AND MINT-CRUSTED LAMB

Use freshly picked parsley and mint from the garden to give a tasty alternative to roast lamb.

2kg/4½ lb leg lamb
a good handful of parsley
a good handful of mint
1 clove of garlic
2 tbsp olive oil
salt & pepper

Put the lamb in the roasting tin and roast on the second set of runners from the top of the roasting oven for 20 minutes per 450g (1lb) plus 20 minutes.

Place the parsley, mint leaves, garlic, oil and salt and pepper in a food processor and chop until fairly smooth.

Thirty minutes before the end of cooking, spread the herb mixture over the lamb. Return to the oven for the remaining time. Allow to 'rest' in a warm place for 10 minutes before carving.

Serves 6–8

PORK CHOPS WITH MUSHROOM AND THYME SAUCE

I know that it is safe to eat pork all year round now, but I still have my cookery teacher's voice ringing in my ears telling me that pork should only be eaten when there is an 'R' in the month. Somehow pork seems to taste better when the weather is cooler. This is a quick recipe that works well when winter turns to spring and meals start to get lighter.

25g/1oz butter
4 pork chops
175g/6oz mushrooms, sliced
1 tbsp chopped thyme
3 tbsp crème fraîche
1 tsp cornflour, blended with a little water
salt & pepper

Melt the butter in the roasting tin and add the chops. Hang the tin on the top set of runners of the roasting oven and cook for 10 minutes. Stir in the mushrooms and thyme, making sure they are coated with butter. Cook for a further 5 minutes and then stir in the crème fraîche and the cornflour mixture.

Place the pan on the floor of the oven for 1–2 minutes until the sauce has thickened. Season and serve immediately.

Serves 4

TURKEY BREAST WITH ASPARAGUS CREAM SAUCE

We used to think of turkey as a Christmas meat only, but it is now available all year round with portions to suit all needs. Combining turkey and asparagus makes a wonderful 'welcome spring' dish. Serve with the new season's potatoes. If you have a shallow cast-iron pan or an ovenproof frying pan, cook this dish on the floor of the roasting oven. Alternatively, cook it on the simmering plate.

225g/8oz asparagus
2 turkey breast fillets, each about 225g/8oz, skinned
2 tbsp seasoned flour
15g/1/2 oz butter
1 tbsp vegetable oil
300ml/1/2
pint chicken or vegetable stock
1 tsp chopped sage
4 tbsp white wine
150ml/1/4 pint soured cream
salt & pepper

Trim the woody end from the asparagus. Cut off the tips and reserve. Cut the remaining stalks into three.

Cut each turkey breast in half. Flatten each portion lightly using a rolling pin and coat in the seasoned flour. Heat the butter and oil in a frying pan and fry the turkey breasts until lightly golden on both sides. Add the stock, asparagus stalks, sage and wine. Cover with a lid or foil and cook gently for 15–20 minutes, until tender. If the turkey is bubbling too quickly, put the shelf on the floor of the oven and place the pan on that.

Five minutes before the end of cooking, add the asparagus tips and stir in the soured cream. Check the seasoning.

Serves 4

LEEK TART

Leeks are one of my favourite vegetables, giving colour and flavour throughout the winter and spring. This recipe is an alternative to a quiche or pastry tart. You will need a large pie dish, or you can use the small roasting tin to make an oblong tart.

250g/9oz strong white flour
1 tsp salt
75g/3oz butter
15g/¹/₂ oz fresh yeast
150ml/¹/₄ pint warm milk
2 eggs, beaten

Filling:
50g/2oz butter
1kg/2lb leeks, sliced
salt & pepper
2 eggs, beaten
150ml/¹/₄ pint double cream

Butter a 23cm (9 inch) pie dish. Put the flour and salt into a large mixing bowl and roughly rub in the butter. Blend the yeast with a little of the warm milk. Add the yeast, eggs and most of the milk to the flour and knead well, adding more milk as necessary to make a soft, pliable dough. Knead well for 5 minutes, then cover with a damp tea-towel and leave to rise for 20–30 minutes, until doubled in size.

Make the filling: melt the butter in a casserole and stir in the leeks. Season and when softening cover with a lid and move to the simmering oven for 30–45 minutes, until the leeks are soft. Beat together the eggs, cream and salt and pepper.

Turn the dough onto a floured work surface and roll to fit the base and sides of the tin. Line the tin with the dough. Pour in the cream mixture. Remove the leeks from the saucepan using a slotted spoon to remove excess moisture. Add to the tart. Stand the tart on a trivet on the simmering plate lid for 15–20 minutes, until the pastry is puffy and the rim has doubled in size.

Bake on the floor of the roasting oven for 30–40 minutes, until the filling is set and the crust is golden-brown.

Serves 6–8

JERSEY ROYAL NEW POTATOES
WITH ASPARAGUS

If you prefer to use just the asparagus tips for this dish, use the remaining portions and the cooking water for soup.

450g/1lb Jersey Royal new potatoes
225g/8oz asparagus

Mint dressing:
1 shallot, chopped
1 tbsp white wine vinegar
50g/2oz butter, diced
2 tbsp single cream
1 tbsp chopped mint
sugar
salt & pepper

Put the potatoes in a saucepan with a heatproof handle, or a casserole dish, with about 2.5cm (1 inch) of water and a pinch of salt. Cover with a lid and bring to the boil. Boil for 1 minute then drain off the water and put the saucepan of potatoes in the simmering oven. The cooking time will depend upon the size of the potatoes and may be anything up to 1 hour. When the potatoes are tender, drain off any excess moisture.

Scrape the stalks of the asparagus and trim the ends. Plunge into boiling, salted water for 8–10 minutes, until the asparagus is tender but not falling apart (the cooking time will depend on the age and size of the stalks). Drain and rinse with cold water.

Make the dressing: place the shallot and wine vinegar in a small saucepan and simmer until the shallot is soft and the vinegar is reduced. Whisk in the butter and cook until the dressing becomes glossy. Whisk in the cream and remove from the heat before adding the mint, a pinch of sugar and salt and pepper.

Put the potatoes in a serving dish and add the asparagus. Pour over the dressing and toss lightly.

Serves 4

ROAST NEW POTATOES WITH ROSEMARY

Freshly dug new potatoes at the beginning of the season need nothing more than scrubbing, boiling with mint and eating with lots of good butter. But later on I often wish to ring the changes. Roast new potatoes are very simple to prepare and go well with grilled meats and fish. I also cook them this way to accompany barbecued food.

450g/1lb new potatoes
2 tbsp olive oil
2 sprigs of rosemary
sea salt

Cut the potatoes, if necessary, so that they are all roughly the same size. Place in the small roasting tin and pour over the oil. Toss well and sprinkle over some salt. Lay on the rosemary. Hang the tin on the top set of runners of the roasting oven and roast for approximately 45–60 minutes, until the potatoes are firm, but cooked through. Remove the rosemary before serving as this can become rather hard and spiky during cooking and not pleasant to eat.

Serves 4

CARROTS WITH MINT AND LEMON

Make this recipe in spring when the first young carrots are available. Choose even-sized carrots so that they cook in the same time and look attractive.

700g/1½ lb small new carrots, scrubbed
salt & pepper
finely grated rind & juice of ½ lemon
1 tsp sugar
15g/½ oz butter
2 tbsp chopped mint

Place the carrots in a saucepan with a heatproof handle. Add about 2.5cm (1 inch) of water. Cover, bring to the boil and then drain off the water. Transfer to the simmering oven for 10–15 minutes, until the carrots are just tender. Drain well and then add the remaining ingredients. Toss together on the boiling plate until the butter melts. Serve immediately.

Serves 4

BAKED SWISS CHARD

Swiss Chard is a useful vegetable in early spring as the green tops can be used like cabbage, or finely shredded for a stir-fry. The thick white stalks can also be shredded for use in stir-fries, or, when they are young, they can be boiled and eaten with melted butter, like asparagus.

1 head of Swiss chard
25g/1oz butter
25g/1oz grated Parmesan

Trim the leaves from the top of the chard and use in a stir-fry or like spinach. Cut each chard stalk in half. Put a pan of salted water onto boil and plunge in the chard. Boil for 8–10 minutes, until tender. Drain well.

Butter an ovenproof dish and put in the chard. Dot with butter and scatter on the Parmesan cheese. Bake at the top of the roasting oven for 15–20 minutes until golden-brown.

Serves 4–6

WATERCRESS PESTO

Traditional Italian pesto is made with basil leaves. Although basil is available in the shops all year round it has a better flavour when it is grown in the summer sun, so that is when I make authentic pesto. During the rest of the year I make watercress pesto to serve on freshly boiled pasta or to use as a sauce for grilled fish.

1 large bunch of watercress
25g/1oz pinenuts
2 cloves of garlic (optional)
5 tbsp olive oil
50g/2oz Parmesan cheese, grated
salt & pepper

Place the watercress, pinenuts and garlic, if using, in a food processor and whizz to a paste.

While the processor is running, slowly add the oil, and then the cheese, salt and pepper. Store in a covered jar in the fridge.

Serves 6

ELDERFLOWER FRITTERS
WITH ELDERFLOWER MOUSSE

Over the last few years elderflower cordial has become a popular non-alcoholic drink which is making us now look at other ways of using those beautiful wayside flowers. These fritters are temptingly light to eat and easy to make. Choose flower heads that have plenty of open flowers, and use them as soon as possible. Pick them in an area away from heavy traffic fumes as they should not be washed before cooking, just shaken to remove any insects.

100g/4oz plain flour
salt
2 tbsp light vegetable oil
150ml/1/4 pint water or lager
1 egg white
oil, for frying
8–12 elderflower heads
icing sugar, for dusting

Elderflower mousse:
250g/9oz mascarpone cheese
2 tbsp elderflower cordial
150ml/1/4 pint double cream,
lightly whipped
2 egg whites
1 tbsp icing sugar, to taste

Place the flour, and salt in a roomy bowl and whisk in the oil and water or lager. Beat to a smooth batter and then cover and leave to stand in a cool place for 1 hour.

Meanwhile, make the mousse: place the mascarpone cheese in a bowl and beat in the cordial. Fold in the cream. Whisk the egg white until stiff but not dry and gently fold into the mousse. Taste and add the icing sugar, if needed. Chill well.

Whisk the egg white until stiff and fold into the batter. Heat oil to a depth of 2cm/³/₄ inch in a large frying pan on the boiling plate. When the oil is hot, holding the stalk, dip each flower head into the batter and drop into the hot oil. Fry until golden-brown and then drain on kitchen paper. Sprinkle with icing sugar and serve on a plate with a scoop of elderflower mousse.

Serves 6–8

RHUBARB CRÊPES

Early rhubarb has a delicate flavour and a beautiful pink blush. If possible, make these fine crêpes in a large cast-iron pan. Get the pan really hot before starting to cook for even cooking and the best crêpes.

450g/1lb rhubarb cut into 2.5cm/1 inch lengths
100g/4oz sugar
175g/6oz plain flour
salt
6 eggs
300ml/1/2 pint milk
3 tbsp rum, brandy or Calvados
75g/3oz butter, melted

Place the rhubarb in a non-metallic bowl and stir in the sugar. Cover and leave to stand for 1 hour. Tip into a saucepan, cover with a lid and bring to the boil on the simmering plate. Transfer to the simmering oven for 30 minutes.

Sift the flour into a mixing bowl with a small pinch of salt. Whisk in the eggs and then the milk. Strain through a sieve into a clean bowl and stir in the rum, brandy or Calvados. Cover and leave to stand for 1 hour.

Stir half the melted butter into the crêpe batter.

Heat the pan on the boiling plate. When hot, brush with melted butter. Pour in a little batter and swirl round to cover the pan. Cook until golden and crisp round the edge, then toss the crêpe and cook the second side for about 1 minute. Continue to cook crêpes until all the batter has been used.

Lay a crêpe onto a plate and spoon on some poached rhubarb. Fold the crêpe into quarters. Dust with a little sugar. Repeat with the remaining crêpes and rhubarb.

Makes 12 crêpes

LEMON TART

I am often asked for this recipe. To get the most flavour and as much juice as possible from lemons, stand them on the hotplate lid handles for a few minutes to warm (if you leave them too long they will start to cook).

225g/8oz sweet shortcrust pastry
100g/4oz unsalted butter
4 lemons
100g/4oz caster sugar
4 eggs

Roll out the pastry and line a 23cm/9 inch flan tin. Chill well.

Put the butter in a mixing bowl and stand at the back of an Aga until the butter has melted. Grate the rind from all the lemons and add to the butter. Thinly slice 1 lemon and set aside.

Squeeze the juice from the remaining lemons and add this to the butter. Whisk the sugar into the butter and lemon mixture and then whisk in the eggs. Pour into the chilled pastry case.

Bake on the floor of the roasting oven for 15 minutes and then lay on the reserved lemon slices and bake for a further 5–10 minutes until set.

Serves 8

RHUBARB CAKE

I am often told how popular my 'German Apple Cake' is that is in *The Traditional Aga Cookery Book*. So here is a springtime variation suggested by my editor, Bron. I added ginger because I think it goes so well with rhubarb, but it can be left out. If you have a glut of rhubarb this recipe freezes very well after baking.

100g/4oz self-raising flour
50g/2oz soft brown sugar
50g/2oz ground almonds
75g/3oz butter, chopped
1 egg, beaten

Filling:
450g/1lb rhubarb,
cut into 2.5cm/1 inch lengths
2 pieces crystallised
ginger, finely chopped

Topping:
100g/4oz self-raising flour
50g/2oz soft brown sugar
1/2 tsp ground ginger
50g/2oz butter, chopped

Butter a 23cm (9 inch) spring-form or other cake tin. Put the self-raising flour, brown sugar and ground almonds in a mixing bowl. Add the butter and rub in until the mixture resembles breadcrumbs. Bind together using the egg. Press the mixture lightly into the base of the tin. Cover the base with the rhubarb and scatter over the ginger.

Make the topping: place the self-raising flour, sugar and ginger in a mixing bowl and rub in the butter until the mixture resembles breadcrumbs. Scatter over the rhubarb.

For a two-oven Aga, place the oven shelf on the floor of the roasting oven. Put in the cake and slide the cold shelf on the second set of runners from the top of the oven. Bake for 1 hour until the topping is golden-brown and the rhubarb is cooked. For a four-oven Aga, place the oven shelf on the second set of runners from the bottom of the baking oven. Bake the cake for about 1 hour until the topping is golden-brown and the rhubarb is cooked.

Serve warm as a pudding or cold as a cake.

Cuts into 8–10 slices

GOOSEBERRY AND RASPBERRY CRUMBLE

Raspberries and gooseberries come into season at about the same time and I often combine them as in this recipe for a perfect spring-time crumble.

450g/1lb gooseberries
225g/8oz raspberries
1 tsp cornflour
sugar, to taste
225g/8oz plain flour
salt
75g/3oz caster sugar
100g/4oz butter, chopped

Place the fruit in an ovenproof dish. Stir together the cornflour and sugar. The amount of sugar depends upon the ripeness of the fruit and your personal taste. Mix the sugar mixture into the fruit.

Place the flour, salt and sugar into a mixing bowl and add the butter. Rub in the butter until the mixture looks like breadcrumbs. Scatter the crumble mixture over the fruit. Bake in the roasting oven with the shelf on the third set of runners from the top for 25–30 minutes, until the crumble is golden-brown and the fruit is just cooked.

Serve with fresh cream.

Serves 4–6

FRUIT KEBABS

Kebabs are often associated with barbecues, but I think cooking them in an Aga brings out the sweetness of the fruit. This is a good way to serve fruits that are available in the markets at the end of spring when they do not have much flavour and are often under-ripe.

1 large pineapple
3 peaches
12 fresh apricots
6 kiwi fruit
icing sugar, for dusting

Soak 12 bamboo skewers in water for about 30 minutes. This makes them easier to put the fruit on and also stops them from charring in the hot oven.

Peel the pineapple and cut into 2.5cm/1 inch dice. Halve the peaches and remove the stones. Cut into 2.5cm/1 inch chunks. Halve the apricots and remove the stones. Peel the kiwi fruit and cut into quarters. Thread the fruits onto the skewers, alternating the fruits.

Line a baking tray with re-usable baking paper, or foil, and lay on the fruit skewers. Dust liberally with icing sugar. Place the baking tray on the highest set of runners possible in the roasting oven and grill for 2–3 minutes, then turn over and dust with icing sugar again. Cook the second side. The sugar should caramelise slightly. Serve hot.

Makes 12

SUMMER

BROAD BEAN AND BACON SOUP

When I was growing up my father grew all our vegetables. Before we had a freezer my brother and I used to joke about 'broad beans for breakfast, lunch and tea'. It was some years after leaving home before I could bring myself to eat broad beans! Their season of June to August is short, so make the most of it. Try to use small beans that haven't yet developed a tough skin.

225g/8oz broad beans, shelled weight
225g/8oz peas, shelled weight
1 large onion, chopped
450ml/3/4 pint milk
300ml/1/2 pint vegetable stock
salt & pepper
2 rashers of bacon, rinds removed

Place the beans, peas, onion, milk and stock in a saucepan with a heatproof handle, or a flameproof casserole, and bring slowly to the boil. Cover and transfer to the simmering oven for 30 minutes. Remove from the oven and pureé half the soup. Mix with the remaining soup and adjust the seasoning.

Place the bacon on a baking tray at the top of the roasting oven to cook for 8–10 minutes and crisp the bacon.

Warm the soup through and crumble or chop the bacon on top.

Serves 4

SPINACH SOUP

Spinach is easy to grow and the young, tender leaves are excellent in salads. Slightly more mature leaves cook in minutes, just in their washing water, and add a wonderful flavour to cheese and fish dishes. Despite all these assets many people are not keen on spinach, but I do find this soup is popular.

25g/1oz butter
1 large onion, chopped
2 tbsp flour
225g/8oz spinach,
thick stalks removed
600ml/1 pint chicken stock
salt & pepper
150ml/1/4 pint single cream
nutmeg

Melt the butter in a saucepan with a heatproof handle, or a flameproof casserole, and fry the onion until soft but not brown. Stir in the flour and cook for 1 minute before adding the spinach. Allow the leaves to wilt and then add the stock and salt and pepper, cover and bring to the boil. When boiling, move to the simmering oven for 30–40 minutes. Purée the spinach mixture and return to the rinsed pan. Check the seasoning, heat through and then ladle into soup bowls. Pour on a little cream and grate on a little nutmeg.

Serves 4

ARTICHOKES WITH TOMATO SAUCE

With an accompaniment of Hollandaise sauce is the standard way of serving artichokes but this truly summer dish makes a delicious variation. Serve hot or at room temperature.

4 shallots, finely chopped
2 tbsp olive oil
4 tomatoes, peeled & chopped
2 tbsp chopped parsley
4 artichokes
salt & pepper
juice 2 lemons

Mix together the shallots, olive oil, tomatoes, parsley and salt and pepper.

Cut the stems and the pointed tops off the artichokes. Soak the artichokes in water acidulated with the lemon juice for 30 minutes. Remove from the water, pull open the centre of each artichoke and remove the hairy choke; this can be done using a sharp spoon or a small knife. Stand the artichokes upright in a flameproof casserole and spoon over the tomato mixture, putting some in the middle of each artichoke. Pour enough water into the dish to come one third of the way up the artichokes. Cover and stand on the simmering plate to bring to the boil. Transfer to the simmering oven for 40–45 minutes, until the artichokes are tender but not mushy.

Serves 4

TOMATO GALETTES

Sometimes in the summer there can be such a glut of tomatoes that you need different ways to serve them. These galettes can be served as a starter or four larger versions made for a main course. If you want a little more substance, add chunks of Feta cheese before the final tomato layer.

250g/9oz puff pastry
75g/3oz sun-dried tomatoes in oil, drained
2 tbsp oil from the tomatoes
basil leaves
6 plum tomatoes, thinly sliced
salt & pepper
olive oil

Roll out the pastry thinly and cut six 8cm/3 inch circles using a cutter or a saucer as a guide. Lay the pastry rounds on a baking tray and prick lightly with a fork. Bake on the second set of runners from the top of the roasting oven for 8–10 minutes, until risen and golden-brown. Cool.

Put the sun-dried tomatoes in a food processor with about 6 basil leaves, salt and pepper and the tomato oil. Whizz. Spread the paste over the pastry rounds. Cover with overlapping circles of sliced tomatoes. Tear over a few more basil leaves and drizzle over a little olive oil.

Bake on the second set of runners from the top of the roasting oven for 5–8 minutes, until the tomato is just softening and tinged black.

Serves 6

ROASTED PEPPERS WITH TOMATOES AND ANCHOVIES

Peppers that are roasted in an Aga have a very sweet flavour. Serve this recipe warm as a starter, or cold as part of a buffet lunch.

4 red peppers
4 tomatoes, skinned & halved
4 cloves of garlic
1 x 25g/1oz can of anchovy fillets, drained
olive oil
a few rosemary leaves (optional)
pepper

Cut the peppers in half from the stalk downwards, leaving the stalks on, if possible, as they make the finished dish more attractive. Remove the seeds. Oil an ovenproof dish and lay in the peppers, cut side uppermost.

Place a tomato half in each pepper half. Divide the garlic among the peppers. Lay the anchovy fillets evenly over the peppers. Scatter on a few rosemary leaves, if using, and grind over some pepper. Drizzle with a little oil.

Put the oven shelf on the second set of runners from the top of the roasting oven and bake the peppers on this shelf for 20–30 minutes, until the peppers are softened and tinged black around the edges. Serve with bread to mop up the juices.

Serves 4 as a starter

TARTE FLAMBÉE

Tarte Flambeé is a good alternative to pizzas. It is delicious eaten straight from the oven but is also good for summer picnics. Grated Gruyère cheese or sliced mushrooms can be added to the topping. For the best results make two or three small tartes rather than one big one; I use Aga baking trays that fit on the oven shelf runners and then I can get two on each shelf level. Alternatively use Swiss roll tins. The tartes should be thin enough to fold slices in half for easy eating.

450g/1lb strong white flour
1½ tsp salt
15g/½oz fresh yeast
about 225ml/8fl oz warm water
1 tbsp oil or melted butter

Topping:
200ml/7fl oz crème fraîche
2 onions, finely sliced
225g/8oz piece of smoked streaky bacon, rinded & diced
pepper

Place the flour and salt in a large mixing bowl. Blend the yeast with a little of the warm water and add to the flour. Then add enough warm water to make a smooth dough that is soft and pliable but not too sticky. Remember that during proving the flour will absorb water, so have the dough as moist as you can handle it at this stage. Knead the dough for 5 minutes and then cover with a damp tea-towel. Leave to rise for about 20 minutes, until doubled in size

Grease 2 baking trays. Knock back the dough and divide in half. Roll each piece to a rectangle slightly larger than a baking tray. The dough will be quite thin. Lift the dough onto the tray.

Spread half the crème fraîche on each dough base, sprinkle over the onion slices and the cubes of bacon. Grind over some black pepper and roll up the edges to make a thin border.

Bake on the second set of runners from the top of the roasting oven for 12–15 minutes, until the top is golden and the base is crisp. If you like a really crisp base then move down to the floor of the roasting oven for 1–2 minutes at the end of cooking.

Makes 2 tartes, each serving 2–3 portions

PAELLA

This simple summer dish is perfect for eating in the garden, served straight from the cooking dish. Fresh seafood can be added according to what you can find fresh that day and to your personal taste. If the seafood is already cooked, add it right at the end of the cooking with just time to heat through.

1kg/2lb chicken, cut into manageable portions
225g/8oz lean pork, roughly diced
salt & pepper
2 tbsp olive oil
1 onion, chopped
2 cloves of garlic, crushed
4 tomatoes, chopped
½ red pepper, seeded & diced
½ green pepper, seeded & diced
100g/4oz green beans, cut into 5cm/2 inch lengths
1.1l/2 pints chicken stock
2 tsp paprika
good pinch of saffron
12 prawns, mussels or snails
225g/8oz risotto or arborio rice
100g/4oz peas

Season the chicken and pork. Heat the oil in a paella pan or very large frying pan and fry the chicken until brown. Add the pork and cook until brown. Now add the onion, garlic, tomatoes, peppers and beans. Cook well and then add the stock, paprika and saffron. If the seafood is raw, add it at this stage. Stir in the rice and bring to the boil. Simmer gently, stirring occasionally, for about 20 minutes, until the rice is cooked. Add the peas and any cooked seafood, check the seasoning and heat through.

Serves 4

SALMON WITH CHAMPAGNE SAUCE

Serve this recipe as a lunch dish in the summer or in smaller portions as a starter, maybe at Christmas-time. It is also a good excuse, if an excuse is needed, to open a bottle of Champagne!

6 salmon fillets
25g/1oz butter
salt & pepper
75ml/3 fl oz white wine
150ml/¼ pint fish stock
150ml/¼ pint champagne
450ml/¾ pint double cream
1 tbsp chopped dill

Salsa:
4 plum tomatoes, seeded & chopped
1 shallot, finely chopped
1 tbsp grated fresh ginger
1–2 tbsp lime juice
pinch of caster sugar
a few basil leaves
salt & pepper

Make the salsa: mix together the tomatoes (for this recipe it is worth the effort to remove the seeds), shallot, ginger, lime juice, sugar, salt and pepper. Then cover and set aside. Tear in the basil leaves just before serving.

Place the salmon fillets in the small roasting tin. Put a knob of butter on each fillet and season with salt and pepper. Add the white wine and 2 tablespoons water. Slide the tin onto the second set of runners from the top of the roasting oven and cook the fish for 8–10 minutes, until the salmon is only just pale pink in the centre.

Meanwhile, pour the stock into a saucepan and bring to the boil. Add the Champagne and, when boiling, whisk in the cream. Boil for

3–4 minutes, until thickened into a sauce. Stir in the dill and check the seasoning.

Divide the sauce among 6 plates, lay a salmon fillet on top and finish with a spoonful of salsa.

Serves 6 as a main course, or 12 as a starter,
cutting each salmon fillet in half.

SEARED TUNA NIÇOISE

This is a salad topped with hot fish. Tuna steaks vary in size and the flesh is very filling, so consider everyone's appetite before you buy.

100g/4oz small new potatoes
100g/4oz French beans
1 red onion, finely chopped
3 plum tomatoes, quartered
12 black olives, pitted
6 anchovy fillets
4 tbsp balsamic vinegar
150ml/1/4 pint olive oil
salt & pepper
2 eggs, hard-boiled & quartered
4 tuna steaks
1 tbsp chopped chives

Cook the potatoes, leave to cool then slice into a roomy bowl. Plunge the beans into a pan of boiling water and cook until just tender but still crisp. Drain and then leave in cold water. When cold, dry and cut into 7.5cm/3 inch lengths.

Add the beans, onion, tomatoes, olives and anchovies to the potatoes.

Put the olive oil and the vinegar in a screw-top jar, season with salt and pepper and put on the lid. Shake well to make a dressing. Moisten the vegetables in the bowl with some of the dressing and then divide the vegetables onto 4 serving plates. Arrange the egg portions on the salads.

Heat a cast-iron ridged pan on the boiling plate or on the floor of the roasting oven for 5 minutes, until really hot. Sear the tuna steaks for about 2 minutes on each side, depending on how you like your fish to be cooked and the thickness of the steaks. Too much cooking will make the fish dry. Place a steak onto each salad and pour over a little more dressing. Sprinkle over the chives.

Serves 4

MACKEREL FISH CAKES WITH APPLE SLICES

Mackerel is a plentiful and economic fish. It is often eaten with a gooseberry sauce (see *The Traditional Aga Cookery Book*, page 49), which is lovely in summer. This is a recipe for people who aren't keen on seeing the whole fish on their plate.

1kg/2lb potatoes
1 cooking apple, peeled, quartered & cored
salt & pepper
25g/1oz butter
3 mackerel, gutted & cleaned
1 egg, beaten
50g/2oz fresh breadcrumbs

For the apples:
4 eating apples, cored
50g/2oz butter

Butter a baking tray well. Put the potatoes, cooking apple, a pinch of salt and 2.5cm/1 inch of water in a saucepan with a heatproof handle. Cover and bring to the boil. Boil for 1 minute then drain off the water and put the pan in the simmering oven for 30–40 minutes until the potatoes are cooked. Drain well and then mash with the butter and salt and pepper. Place the mackerel on the rack inside the roasting tin (the small one should be large enough) and grill the mackerel at the top of the roasting oven for 5 minutes on each side. Remove the fish from the oven and, when it is cool enough to handle, discard the skin and bones and flake the fish. Carefully mix the potatoes with the mackerel. If the mixture is very stiff, add a drop of milk, but do not make it at all sloppy. Shape into 8 fish cakes.

Put the beaten egg onto a plate and the breadcrumbs onto a separate plate. Dip each fish cake in the egg and then in the breadcrumbs. Place the fish cakes on the baking tray and on the floor of the roasting oven. Cook the fish cakes for 10 minutes, then turn them over and crisp the other side.

Meanwhile prepare the apples. Peel the apples if the skin is tough. Slice them horizontally into 4 apple rings. Heat the butter in a frying pan until it is frothing, then fry the apple slices in batches.

Serve the fish cakes immediately with the apple slices.

Makes 8 fish cakes

SQUID PROVENÇAL

Squid is available all year round, but this is a wonderful way of cooking it quickly in the summer. Cleaning squid can take a little time, but most fishmongers will do it for you.

1 tbsp olive oil
1 onion, chopped
450g/1lb squid, cleaned & sliced
1 clove of garlic, crushed
1 courgette, quartered & diced
1/2 red pepper, seeded & chopped
2 tomatoes, peeled & chopped
salt & pepper
1 tbsp chopped parsley

Heat the olive oil in a frying pan and add the onion. Cook until softening but not browning. Add the squid and garlic, stir well and then add the courgette and pepper. Cook for 1–2 minutes before stirring in the tomatoes. Cook until the tomatoes are beginning to 'fall'. Season with salt and pepper and parsley.

Serve immediately.

Serves 2

CHICKEN AND BACON ROLLS WITH GARLIC DIP

The rolls can be served as a starter, sliced onto a bed of salad, but I like them served with a garlic dip, roast new potatoes and plenty of summer salad. We have made these rolls on children's cookery days; stretching the bacon seems fun, but it is only second best to eating the chicken with fingers and dipping it into the garlic dip. The small roasting tin and rack may be a little small for this number of chicken pieces. It may be better to use the large roasting tin.

12 boneless & skinless chicken thighs
2 tbsp grain mustard
12 rashers streaky bacon, rinds removed

Garlic dip:
3 tbsp mayonnaise
3 tbsp fromage frais
2 cloves garlic, crushed

To make the garlic dip: mix the ingredients together and chill before serving.

Unroll each chicken thigh and spread on a little mustard. Re-roll the thighs. Gently stretch the rashers of bacon with a table knife. Wrap 1 rasher round each chicken thigh and secure with a wooden cocktail stick. Place the chicken on the rack set inside the roasting tin. Hang the tin on the second set of runners of the roasting oven and bake for 35–40 minutes, until the chicken is golden-brown and the juices run clear when the chicken is pierced.

Makes 12

WARM CHICKEN SALAD

A quick and simple lunch or supper dish for hot summer days when you don't want to slave over a hot Aga. Have everything prepared in advance and cook the chicken at the last minute.

4 boneless & skinless chicken portions,
shredded as for a stir-fry
4 spring onions, chopped
1 tbsp olive oil
50g/2oz flaked almonds
mixed salad leaves, to serve

Dressing:
2 tbsp balsamic vinegar
3 tbsp olive oil
2 tbsp single cream
1 tsp mustard
pinch of sugar
salt & pepper

Make the dressing: place all the ingredients in a screw-top jar, put on the lid and shake well.

Divide the salad leaves among 4 plates.

Heat the oil in a large frying pan and stir in the chicken and the spring onions. Cook, stirring most of the time, until the onions are soft but not brown and the chicken strips are cooked through. Pour over the dressing and remove from the heat. Scatter over the flaked almonds and divide the chicken among the plates of salad.

Serve immediately.

Serves 4

SUMMER CHICKEN TART

The addition of crème fraîche to the filling gives this tart a more substantial texture than a quiche. It can be eaten warm or cold, so it is useful for picnics or outdoor eating.

225g/8oz shortcrust pastry
2 tbsp olive oil
2 large boneless & skinless chicken breasts, sliced
1 red pepper, seeded & finely sliced
1 green pepper, seeded & finely sliced
1 clove of garlic, crushed
2–3 sprigs of thyme
225ml/8fl oz crème fraîche
2 eggs, beaten
150ml/¼ pint milk
25g/1oz Parmesan cheese, grated
salt & pepper
a few black & green olives, pitted & halved
5 sun-dried tomatoes, quartered

Roll out the pastry to line a 23cm/9 inch flan tin. Chill.

Heat the olive oil in a large frying pan and cook the chicken for 2–3 minutes, stirring frequently. Add the peppers, garlic and thyme and fry until the chicken is cooked through and the peppers are tender but still retain some 'bite'. Remove the thyme and allow the pan mixture to cool a little.

Beat together the crème fraîche, eggs, milk, Parmesan cheese and salt and pepper. Spread the chicken and pepper mixture over the pastry case, pour over the crème fraîche mixture and scatter over the olives and sun-dried tomatoes.

Bake on the floor of the roasting oven for 25–30 minutes, until set and lightly golden.

Serves 6

CHICKEN TIKKA SKEWERS

Chicken tikka is said to be one of Britain's favourite dishes. I'm not so sure about that but I do know that these chicken tikka skewers are popular. I like a helping of onion chutney as well.

4 large boneless & skinless chicken breasts,
cut into 2.5cm/1 inch chunks
juice of 2 lemons
salt
100g/4oz plain yoghurt
25g/1oz chilli paste
1 tsp ground coriander
1 tsp garam masala
1 tsp crushed garlic
1 tsp chopped fresh ginger
1/2 tsp turmeric
vegetable oil

Put the chicken in a non-metallic dish and sprinkle with the lemon juice and salt.

Mix together the yoghurt, chilli paste, coriander, garam masala, garlic, ginger and turmeric. Pour over the chicken and leave to marinate for at least 2 hours.

Thread the chicken onto skewers or bamboo sticks, and brush with a little oil. Place on a rack inside the large roasting tin. Allow some space between the skewers so that the meat can cook evenly.

Slide the tin onto the second set of runners from the top of the roasting oven and cook for about 15 minutes, turning once. Take care not to cook for too long otherwise the meat will become too dry.

Serves 4

CHICKEN GOUJONS WITH TOMATO VINAIGRETTE

For a quick and simple way of adding interest to chicken breasts I wrap the pieces of chicken in air-dried ham and serve them on a bed of salad leaves with a tomato vinaigrette. I like to serve the goujons warm, but if you prefer, chill them before serving.

3 boneless & skinless chicken breasts
100g/4oz air-dried ham
a selection of salad leaves
2 tbsp tomato purée
4 tbsp olive oil
2 tbsp red wine vinegar
salt & pepper
pinch of sugar
6 basil leaves

Cut each chicken breast into 4 strips. Wrap each strip in a piece of air-dried ham and lay in the small roasting tin. Hang the tin on the second set of runners from the top of the roasting oven and roast for 15–20 minutes, until the meat is crisp and the chicken is cooked.

While the chicken is cooking, divide the salad leaves among 4 plates.

Place the tomato purée, olive oil, wine vinegar, salt and pepper and a pinch of sugar in a screw-top jar. Put on the lid and shake well to emulsify the ingredients. Tear up the basil leaves and add just before serving.

When the chicken is cooked, lift each piece onto a chopping board and slice into pieces about 2.5cm/1 inch thick. Put the chicken on the salad leaves and drizzle over the vinaigrette.

Serves 4

CHICKEN AND GREEN BEAN GRATIN

This is a good way to use left-over cooked chicken in the summer when fresh green beans are available. Any hard cheese will work well but Red Leicester or Double Gloucester give the sauce a lovely colour.

40g/1½ oz butter
40g/1½ oz flour
600ml (1 pint) milk
75g/3oz Red Leicester, grated
½ tsp mustard
salt & pepper
450g/1lb cooked chicken, skinned & cubed
450g/1lb green beans, lightly cooked
50g/2oz dried apricots, preferably 'no-soak', chopped
25g/1oz flaked almonds

Put the butter, flour and milk in a saucepan and place on the simmering plate. Bring to the boil, whisking all the time with a wire whisk until thickened to a glossy sauce. Remove from the heat and whisk in the cheese, mustard and salt and pepper.

Butter an ovenproof dish and put in the chicken, beans and apricots. Pour over the sauce and sprinkle on the almonds.

Place the oven shelf on the third set of runners from the top of the roasting oven. Slide in the prepared dish and bake for 20–25 minutes, until bubbling hot and the nuts are golden-brown.

Serves 4

CHICKEN WITH TARRAGON MAYONNAISE

This is a perfect summer dish using fresh tarragon; I'm afraid that dried tarragon will not work as well. I have specified chicken breasts but you could poach a whole chicken and use the meat from that.

6 chicken breast fillets, skinned
2 sticks of celery, sliced
200ml/7fl oz white wine
2 tbsp & 2 tsp chopped tarragon
salt & pepper
300ml/½ pint mayonnaise

Place the chicken in a shallow, ovenproof dish with the celery, white wine, 2 tablespoons of tarragon and salt and pepper. Cover with a lid or foil.

Put the oven shelf on the second set of runners from the bottom of the roasting oven and slide in the chicken dish. Poach the chicken for 30–40 minutes, until tender. Remove the chicken to a plate and allow to cool. Pour the cooking juices into a small saucepan and boil to reduce to 4 tablespoons. Cool completely.

Strain the reduced liquid into the mayonnaise and add the remaining tarragon. Slice the chicken breasts onto a serving plate and spoon over the tarragon mayonnaise.

Serves 6

SHISH KEBABS

Shish kebabs make a good addition to a summer buffet lunch, served with salads, chutneys and pitta breads. They can also be taken on a picnic, for eating cold.

700g/1½ lb rump steak
225g/8oz onion
2 red chillies, seeded
2 tbsp roughly chopped coriander
2.5cm/1 inch piece of fresh root ginger, roughly chopped
1 tsp garam masala
salt & pepper
½ tsp ground cloves
½ tsp ground cinnamon
½ tsp cumin
½ tsp grated nutmeg
vegetable oil

Place all the ingredients except the oil in a food processor or a mincer and mince to a fine paste.

Oil your hands and divide the mixture into 8 portions. Mould each portion round a skewer, making a sausage shape.

Stand the rack inside the small roasting tin and lay on the kebabs. Slide the tin onto the highest set of runners of the roasting oven, but without the meat touching the top of the oven, and grill for 10 minutes. Turn over and cook for a further 5 minutes.

Makes 8

PIGEON AND PEACH SALAD WITH HAZELNUT DRESSING

Pigeons are the smallest and cheapest of all the game birds, and are at their best between May and October, so summer peaches make a good accompaniment. Pigeon breasts are now so popular that you may have to order them from your butcher. If you buy whole birds you will need one bird per person.

8 pigeon breasts, skinned
salt & pepper
1 tbsp hazelnut oil
4 peaches
salad leaves
50g/2oz hazelnuts, roasted & chopped

Dressing:
2 tbsp hazelnut oil
4 tbsp sunflower oil
2 tbsp wine vinegar
salt & pepper

Make the dressing: put the oils, vinegar and salt and pepper into a screw-top jar and put on the lid. Shake well.

Heat a heavy, large frying pan until really hot. Season the pigeon breasts. Add the oil to the hot pan and then fry the pigeon breasts for about 2 minutes on each side until brown on the outside but pink in the middle. Remove from the pan and allow to cool.

Put the salad leaves on serving plates. Cut each peach into 8 slices and place on the salad leaves. Slice the cooked pigeon and add to the salad leaves. Scatter over the hazelnuts and pour on the vinaigrette dressing.

Serves 4

SPINACH QUICHE

Spinach seems to be an undervalued vegetable. Baby leaves make a delicious salad with crisp bacon, but this recipe uses larger leaves.

450g/1lb fresh spinach leaves
4 rashers of streaky bacon, rinds removed
225g/8oz shortcrust pastry
25g/1oz pine nuts
3 eggs
150ml/¼ pint milk
150ml/¼ pint cream
grated nutmeg
salt

Wash the spinach leaves well and remove any thick stalks. Place in a pan with just the washing water clinging to the leaves. Cover with a lid and place on the simmering plate for 8–10 minutes, until the leaves have collapsed. Drain off any excess moisture and chop well.

Place the rashers of bacon on a baking tray and put towards the top of the roasting oven for 10–15 minutes, until crisp. Leave until cool enough to handle, then crumble the bacon and set aside.

Use the pastry to line a 23cm/9 inch shallow flan tin. Spread the spinach over the base. Scatter on the pine nuts. Beat together the eggs, milk, cream, nutmeg and salt. Pour onto the spinach and sprinkle with the crumbled bacon.

Place the quiche on the floor of the roasting oven for 20–25 minutes, until the filling is set.

Serves 4–6

SUMMER VEGETABLE FLAN

This flan is perfect when all the summer vegetables are in the garden and can be made with vegetable thinnings from the main crops. The nutty pastry gives the finished dish an interesting texture.

175g/6oz plain flour
75g/3oz butter
salt & pepper
50g/2oz walnuts, toasted & coarsely ground

Filling:
25g/1oz butter
175g/6oz courgettes, cut into sticks
1 clove of garlic, crushed
175g/6oz thin asparagus
175g/6oz carrots, cut into sticks
50g/2oz peas
1 egg yolk
4 tomatoes, peeled & finely chopped
100g/4oz cream cheese
150ml/¼ pint single cream
2 eggs, beaten
2 tbsp chopped mixed herbs
salt & pepper
50g/2oz Gruyère or mature Cheddar cheese, grated

Put the flour and salt in a bowl. Add the butter and rub into the flour until the mixture resembles breadcrumbs. Stir in the ground walnuts. Bind to a firm dough with cold water. Roll out to fit a 23cm/9 inch flan tin. Chill.

Make the filling: heat the butter in a frying pan and fry the courgettes until softening and then add the garlic. Fry until just colouring. Drain from the pan. Blanch the asparagus, carrot sticks and peas in boiling water for 2 minutes. Drain and plunge into cold water. Drain.

Brush the pastry case with egg yolk and then scatter over the tomatoes.

Lay the prepared vegetables on top. Beat together any remaining egg yolk, the eggs, cream cheese, cream, herbs and salt and pepper. Pour over the vegetables. Sprinkle over the grated cheese.

Bake on the floor of the roasting oven for 25–30 minutes, until the filling is set and golden-brown on the top.

Serves 6

Couscous with Roast Summer Vegetables and Goats' Cheese

Many different vegetables can be used for this dish, such as aubergines and courgettes. If you end up cooking too many vegetables, reserve the extras, toss in salad dressing and serve cold as a starter, or mix with Feta cheese as a light lunch dish.

8 plum tomatoes, halved
1 red onion, quartered
2 red peppers, seeded & cut into chunks
1 red chilli, seeded & halved
4 cloves of garlic, peeled
2–3 sprigs of thyme
3 tbsp olive oil
1 tbsp balsamic vinegar
salt & pepper
300g/10oz couscous
600ml/1 pint hot vegetable stock
2 tbsp herbs, finely chopped
100g/4 oz goats' cheese, rind removed & diced

Line the small roasting tin with re-usable baking paper or foil. Put the tomatoes, onion, peppers, chilli, garlic and thyme into the tin. Season with salt and pepper and drizzle over the oil and vinegar. Hang on the top set of runners of the roasting oven for 30–40 minutes, until the vegetables are tender but not mushy. They may tinge with colour in this time. If your Aga cooks quickly, keep an eye on the vegetables to make sure the onions don't blacken.

Place the couscous in a heatproof bowl and pour on the hot vegetable stock. Cover with a lid or a plate and stand at the back of the Aga for about 20 minutes, until the stock has been absorbed.

Place half the vegetables in a food processor, process and then pass

through a sieve. If you do not like a hot sauce, remove the chilli before processing. Taste and adjust the seasoning.

Stir the herbs into the couscous and pile onto a large serving plate. Pour over the sauce and pile on the remaining roast vegetables. Scatter over the goats' cheese.

Serves 4

PINK FIR APPLE POTATO SALAD

My father used to grow the wonderful pink fir apple salad potatoes long before they were available in supermarkets. We had different varieties of potatoes all the year round and pink fir apple is one of my favourites; they cannot be peeled, just give them a good scrub.

700g/1½ lb pink fir apple potatoes
salt
1 sprig of mint

Dressing:
2 tbsp olive oil
grated rind & juice of 1 lemon
1 tsp Dijon mustard
1 tbsp white wine vinegar
salt & pepper
chopped chives

Cut the potatoes into roughly even sizes. Place in a saucepan with a heatproof handle, or a flameproof casserole, with 4cm/1½ inches of water, a sprig of mint and a pinch of salt. Cover and bring to the boil. Boil for 1 minute and then drain off the water. Re-cover and put the pan with the potatoes in the simmering oven for 30 minutes. Test the potatoes with a sharp knife to see if they are cooked. Drain well.

Make the dressing: put the oil, lemon rind and juice, mustard, wine vinegar and salt and pepper in a screw-top jar. Put on the lid and shake well until emulsified. Pour over the warm potatoes. Sprinkle with chopped chives and serve warm or cold.

Serves 4

GRILLED FENNEL WITH FETA

The fennel used for salads or cooking as a vegetable is the swollen bulb of Florence fennel. The leaves can be cut and used as a garnish. Fennel has a distinctive aniseed flavour and is good sliced into summer salads. Alternatively, it can be quartered and baked and covered in a cheese sauce. This recipe is good served as a starter or as a salad with cold meats and cheeses.

3 fennel bulbs
a little olive oil for brushing
4 tbsp olive oil
2 tbsp lemon juice
salt & pepper
150g/5oz Feta cheese
a few black olives

Trim the feathery leaves from the top of the fennel. Trim the root end. Remove any outer layers that look bruised or tough (use them for stock or soup). Bring a pan of water to the boil and add the fennel bulbs. Simmer for 5 minutes, drain and then plunge into cold water to cool. Drain. Cut each bulb into quarters from the top to the root. Brush with olive oil and lay on the rack set inside the small roasting tin. Hang on the second set of runners from the top of the roasting oven and grill for 10 minutes, until starting to brown.

Whisk together the olive oil, lemon juice and salt and pepper. Put the grilled fennel in a serving dish and pour over the dressing. Break the Feta over the fennel and add the olives. Serve warm or chilled.

Serves 6

CARAMELISED PINEAPPLE WITH RASPBERRIES

At the start of the raspberry season you may need to find a way to make a few berries go a long way, and yet still enjoy the flavour. Pineapple works well with raspberries and they are usually reasonably priced at the start of the raspberry season.

1 pineapple
2 tbsp icing sugar
175g/6oz raspberries

Remove the skin of the pineapple with a sharp knife and cut the fruit into 8 slices. Remove the core; I do this with a cocktail cutter.

Heat a ridged pan or a heavy frying pan on the boiling plate for 8–10 minutes until really hot.

Dust the pineapple with icing sugar on one side and place in the pan, sugared side down. Dust the upper side with sugar and turn over. There should be caramelised ridges in the pineapple.

Serve the pineapple garnished with the raspberries.

Serves 4

CHERRY CRUMBLE TART

The home-grown cherry season is very short, at the height of the summer. Cherries are delicious in fruit salads or in bowls of fruit with Ricotta cheese and sugar. However, if you are lucky enough to have a glut of cherries, this tart will do them justice. I know that removing the stones from cherries is a chore but it will make life easier when eating the tart. Canned or bottled cherries can be substituted.

1kg/2lb cherries, stones removed
Or 2 x 425g/15oz canned or bottled cherries
50g/2oz sugar
2 tbsp cornflour

Pastry:
225g/8oz plain flour
50g/2oz caster sugar
pinch of salt
100g/4oz butter, chopped
1 egg, beaten

Crumble topping:
50g/2oz flour
50g/2oz caster sugar
1/4 tsp cinnamon
50g/2oz chopped almonds

Make the pastry: put the flour, salt and sugar into a mixing bowl. Add the butter and rub in until the mixture looks like breadcrumbs. Add the egg to bind the pastry together, adding cold water if necessary. As the pastry rests it will absorb moisture so make sure that the pastry is not too dry at this stage. Wrap in cling film and allow to rest, but do not chill.

If the cherries are fresh, put them in a shallow pan with the sugar and enough water to come about 1.5cm/1/4 inch up the sides of the pan. Cook gently until softening. Drain the juice from the cherries, whether fresh or canned. Blend 100ml/1/2 pint of juice with the cornflour.

Pour into a small saucepan and bring to the boil until thickening. Stir into the cherries and allow to cool.

Make the crumble topping: place the flour, sugar and cinnamon in a bowl and rub in the butter. When the mixture resembles bread-crumbs, stir in the almonds.

Roll the pastry to fit a 23cm/9 inch loose-based flan tin. When lined, spoon in the cherries and then cover with the crumble topping. Bake on the floor of the roasting oven for 25–30 minutes, until the topping is golden-brown and the pastry is crisp and dry.

Serves 6–8

APRICOT AND CHERRY CRUMBLE

Having bought a lot of fruit one day from a market stall in London, I had to decide how best to prepare it because it wouldn't keep for long after a train journey home. If you prefer a juicier crumble, omit the ground rice, which helps to thicken the juices.

450g/1lb apricots, quartered & stones removed
450g/1lb cherries, stones removed
1 tbsp ground rice
1 tbsp sugar

Crumble:
100g/4oz plain flour
50g/2oz butter
25g/1oz caster sugar
salt

Put the apricots and cherries in a mixing bowl. Mix together the ground rice and sugar and then stir into the fruit. Tip into an oven-proof baking dish or fill 6 ramekin dishes.

Make the crumble: place the flour, butter, caster sugar and a pinch of salt in a mixing bowl and rub in the butter to resemble fine breadcrumbs. Scatter the crumble mixture over the fruit. Bake on the second set of runners from the bottom of the roasting oven for 20–25 minutes, until the fruit is just soft and the crumble is golden-brown.

Serves 6

PEACH AND MARZIPAN SLICE

One day when I had plenty of peaches that wouldn't ripen before rotting I created this simple pudding. Firm plums or apricots can also be used.

425g/15oz ready-rolled puff pastry
50g/2oz marzipan
6 peaches, halved & stones removed
1 tbsp caster sugar

Unroll the pastry onto a baking tray. Divide the marzipan into 12 portions and put 1 portion into the stone cavity of each peach. Place each peach half on the pastry, cut side down. Sprinkle over the caster sugar.

Bake on the second set of runners from the top of the roasting oven for 15 minutes, until the pastry is risen and golden around the peaches. Move to the floor of the oven for 5 minutes to crisp the base. Serve immediately.

Serves 6

SUMMER FRUIT TORTE

A summer fruit torte is an ideal recipe for when you have a selection of soft summer fruits. It also helps a little fruit to go a long way and still give a taste of summer.

300g/10oz plain flour
salt
150g/5oz butter
50g/2oz caster sugar
1 egg, beaten
cold water

Filling:
450g/1lb soft summer fruits
icing sugar, for dusting

Place the flour, salt, butter and sugar in a food processor or mixer and process until the mixture is like fine breadcrumbs. Take out 3 tablespoons of crumble mixture and set aside. Add the egg and enough cold water to bind the mixture together to form a dough. Roll out to fit a shallow 23cm/9 inch flan tin. Chill.

Scatter the summer fruits over the pastry case. Sprinkle on the reserved crumble mixture.

Bake on the floor of the roasting oven for 20–25 minutes, until golden-brown and the fruit is soft. Dust with icing sugar.

Serves 6

RASPBERRY CHEESECAKE

I make this baked cheesecake using either raspberries or blueberries: a good layer of fresh fruit on the top makes a delicious dessert. The fruit keeps its shape better if it is frozen before it is added to cheese mixture. Make the cheesecake the day before you want to serve it because it is easier to cut after chilling.

1 box of trifle sponges, slit in half
450g/1lb low-fat curd cheese, such as Quark
50g/2oz caster sugar
2 tbsp cornflour
salt
2 eggs, beaten
1 egg yolk
grated rind of 1 lemon
300ml/$1/_2$ pint double cream
100g/4oz frozen raspberries
fresh fruit, to serve

Butter the base and side of a 23cm/9 inch spring-release cake tin. Line the base with the trifle sponges, making sure there are no gaps.

Mix together the cheese, sugar, cornflour, salt, eggs, egg yolk, lemon rind and cream. When well mixed, gently fold in the frozen fruit. Pour the cheese mixture carefully over the sponge base and level the surface.

For a two-oven Aga: put the shelf on the floor of the roasting oven, put in the cheesecake and slide the cold shelf one runner above the top of the tin.

For a four-oven Aga: put the oven shelf on the second set of runners from the bottom of the baking oven and put in the cheesecake.

Bake for 40–50 minutes, until set. After 30 minutes check to see if the top is becoming brown; if it is, place a sheet of foil loosely over the top, to prevent browning.

Cool completely in the tin then chill well before serving. Decorate with fresh fruit.

Cut into 8–10 slices

RASPBERRY AND STRAWBERRY MILLE-FEUILLE

A triple-layer dish always looks spectacular yet is very easy to prepare, so it is perfect for a summer dessert. Fill with a good layer of ripe raspberries and strawberries. If you like, you can make individual portions: simply mark and cut the pastry into narrower widths before and after baking. Ready-rolled puff pastry works particularly well for this recipe as it will rise perfectly evenly, unlike some hand-rolled pastry.

375g/13oz ready-rolled puff pastry
450ml/³/₄ pint double cream
1 tbsp fruit liqueur (e.g. framboise)
350g/12oz raspberries & strawberries, mixed
icing sugar, for dusting

Unroll the pastry and lay on a baking tray. Mark into 3 even portions with a knife, but do not cut right through the pastry. Bake on the second set of runners from the top of the roasting oven for 15 minutes. Remove and turn the tray round and bake for a further 5 minutes, until risen and evenly golden-brown. Take from the oven and cut through the knife markings to make 3 equal portions. Transfer to a cooling rack until completely cold.

Whip the cream and liqueur together until thick and just holding peaks. (In warm weather take care not to over-whip the cream and make it grainy.) Slice the strawberries if they are large so that they are the same thickness as the raspberries.

Place a portion of pastry on a plate and cover with half the cream and half the fruit. Place a second sheet of pastry on top of the fruit and cover with the remaining cream and the fruit. Top with the remaining portion of pastry and dust with a good layer of icing sugar.

Heat several metal skewers under the lid of the boiling plate, (remember to use an oven cloth to remove them for use). When the skewers are red hot lay them over the surface of the mille-feuille to make a diamond pattern by caramelising the icing sugar. Serve well chilled.

Serves 6

BLACKCURRANT SLUMP

'Slump' seems a funny name for a pudding, but it is really a cobbler that has gone wrong! The filling should be fairly soft to allow the scone topping to fall into the filling and become soft. I have adapted my mother's recipe to use mascarpone cheese instead of thick double cream; use whichever you prefer.

700g/1½lb blackcurrants, off the stalk
3 tbsp water
sugar to taste
1 tbsp cornflour, blended with a little water
250g/9oz mascarpone cheese

Scone topping:
175g/6oz self-raising flour
1 tsp baking powder
pinch of salt
50g/2oz sugar
50g/2oz butter, chopped
75ml/3fl oz milk

Place the fruit in a saucepan with the water, and sugar to taste. Bring to the boil and add the slaked cornflour. Stir well and cook for 2–3 minutes, until the fruit is cooked but not mushy. Pour into an oven-proof dish that has enough room for the scone mix on top. Place spoonfuls of mascarpone on top of the fruit, but do not stir in.

Make the scone topping: place the flour, baking powder, salt, sugar and butter in a mixing bowl and rub in the butter. Bind together with the milk, adding more if necessary to form a soft dough. Place spoonfuls of the dough on top of the fruit.

Put the oven shelf on the bottom set of runners of the roasting oven and bake the slump for 25–30 minutes, until the scone is golden-brown and the fruit is bubbling.

Serves 6

BLACKCURRANT CLAFOUTIS

A clafoutis is a traditional baked batter dish from Limousin in France, made with cherries. As blackcurrants are more plentiful in this country I usually use them instead of cherries.

450g/1lb blackcurrants, weighed off the stalks
3 tbsp plain flour
3 tbsp caster sugar
3 eggs
300ml/¹/₂ pint milk
caster sugar, for dusting

Butter a shallow, ovenproof dish very well and scatter the blackcurrants over the base.

Put the flour and sugar in a mixing bowl. Add the eggs and gradually whisk in the milk to make a smooth batter. Pour the batter over the fruit.

Put the oven shelf on the second set of runners from the top of the roasting oven and slide in the clafoutis. Bake for 30–40 minutes, until risen and golden-brown.

Note: This recipe needs a hot oven, so, like Yorkshire puddings, cook it before using the oven for other baking.

Serves 6

SWIRLY PAVLOVA
WITH STRAWBERRIES

Swirls of chocolate meringue in the plain meringue make a change and taste really good with strawberries (or raspberries, if you prefer). The chocolate meringue remains a little more moist and chewy than the plain meringue. If you want to make the meringue bases several days ahead of serving, dry them out for an hour or two longer in the simmering oven and store in an airtight container. Add the filling 1 hour before serving to allow the meringue to moisten.

2 tbsp icing sugar
2 tbsp cocoa
4 egg whites
225g/8oz caster sugar
350g/12oz strawberries
300ml/¹/₂ pint double cream, whipped

Line the cold shelf with re-usable baking paper or baking parchment. Mix together the icing sugar and cocoa powder. Whisk the egg whites in a clean, dry, grease-free bowl until they are white and fluffy. Continue to whisk, adding the caster sugar 1 teaspoonful at a time. Spoon half the meringue mixture into a circle on the cold shelf, leaving a few gaps for the chocolate meringue. Now slowly whisk the cocoa mixture into the other half of the meringue. Spoon this onto the cold shelf, filling in the circles of meringue. Take a table knife and cut through the meringues to form a swirled effect, taking care not to over-mix the meringues.

Bake on the middle set of runners of the simmering oven for 3–4 hours, until the meringue is crisp on the outside and moist in the middle. Cool on a wire rack.

Stand the meringue on a serving plate. Fold half the strawberries into the cream. Pile onto the meringue. Finish with the remaining strawberries.

Serves 6–8

BLUEBERRY MUFFINS

I have adapted this recipe from an American recipe that was given to me by Aga owners in the States. British blueberries can be found in markets from July to October and are lovely eaten fresh in fruit salads, or lightly poached in a fruit compôte. However, imported blueberries have a much longer season and they can also often be found in the frozen food department of good supermarkets. For this recipe, freeze the blueberries before putting into the muffin mixture to prevent the muffins turning completely blue.

450g/1lb plain flour
175g/6oz sugar
salt
4 tsp baking powder
2 eggs, beaten
100ml/4fl oz light vegetable oil
225ml/8fl oz milk
225g/8oz frozen blueberries

Mix together the flour, sugar, salt and baking powder. Stir the eggs, vegetable oil and milk together. Add the egg mixture to the flour, mix lightly, then stir in the frozen blueberries. Make sure there is no loose flour at the bottom of the mixing bowl.

Line 12 deep muffin tins with paper cases and three-quarters fill with the muffin mixture.

Put the oven shelf on the third set of runners from the top of the roasting oven, slide in the muffins and bake for 15–20 minutes until golden-brown, risen and firm to the touch. Eat on the day of baking, or freeze and warm through as required.

Makes 12

BISCOTTI

Italian Biscotti are great for dunking into coffee, but very expensive to buy. Biscotti are much cheaper and are very simple to make at home, and they taste better. I serve them with summer fruit compôtes; dipped in their juices they are delicious. They keep very well in an air-tight tin.

100g/4oz whole, blanched almonds or hazelnuts
175g/6oz plain flour
1/2 tsp baking powder
175g/6oz caster sugar
salt
2 eggs, beaten
1 tsp vanilla essence

Spread the nuts on a baking tray and put on the top set of runners of the roasting oven for about 4 minutes. Remove from the oven and if not evenly toasted turn the tray round and return to the oven for 2 minutes more. Cool the toasted nuts. If your Aga is 'hot' the nuts may toast more quickly, so watch them.

Place the flour, baking powder, sugar and salt in a mixing bowl. Lightly stir in the eggs and vanilla essence and then the cooled nuts. Gently mix the dough together and divide in half.

Line a large baking tray with re-usable baking paper. Place the 2 pieces of dough side by side on the baking tray and pat out to a sausage shape, about 20cm/8 inches long. The mixture will spread during cooking.

For a two-oven Aga: put the shelf on the bottom set of runners of the roasting oven, put in the biscotti and slide the cold shelf onto the second set of runners from the top of the oven.

For a four-oven Aga: bake on the third set of runners from the top of the baking oven. Bake for 20 minutes, until pale gold and just firm to the touch. Remove from the oven and cool for 10 minutes. Lift onto a chopping board and cut into slices about 2cm/3/4 inch thick. Return to the baking tray and then to the oven as above for 8–10 minutes. Cool on a wire rack.

DRIED TOMATO CRISPS

This is a way of making you own 'sun-dried tomatoes' to use either in dishes calling for them, or to serve as nibbles with drinks. If the tomato crisps are to be used for cooking, you can store them in olive oil. Simply allow the tomatoes to become cold after drying, pack into a clean jar and cover with oil and seal. Any type of tomato can be dried and they will each give a different flavour. The riper the tomatoes the sweeter the dried tomatoes will be.

ripe tomatoes
salt

Line the large roasting tin with re-usable baking paper, or foil. Slice the tomatoes into rounds about 5mm/¼ inch thick and lay in a single layer in the tin. Slide the tray onto the middle set of runners of the simmering oven and dry for 4–5 hours (if you are doing cherry tomatoes, cut them in half and they may dry in 3 hours). The drying time will depend upon the ripeness of the tomatoes and the warmth of your simmering oven, so keep an eye on the tomatoes.

Cool completely before storing in an airtight container.

AUTUMN

CELERY SOUP
WITH CHEESE TOPPING

We had a run of celery in the weekly vegetable box. This 'bumpy stuff', as my children call celery, is not a popular vegetable with them, but they do eat soup. So a way to disguise the main ingredient in this soup is to top it with Emmental cheese, which melts easily and adds a luscious layer as you eat.

25g/1oz butter
1 head of celery, chopped
1 onion, chopped
25g/1oz flour
1l/1³/₄ pints
chicken or vegetable stock
salt & pepper
75g/3oz Emmental cheese, grated

Melt the butter in a saucepan with a heatproof handle, or a flame-proof casserole, and add the celery and onion and fry until softening, but not browning. Stir in the flour and cook for 1–2 minutes before gradually stirring in the stock. Bring to the boil and then cover and transfer to the simmering oven for 45 minutes.

Remove from the oven and purée the soup. Check the seasoning, heat through and ladle into warm soup bowls. Sprinkle over the grated cheese.

Serves 6

PUMPKIN SOUP

Pumpkins and squashes are often used solely for decoration, but their flesh can be roasted or tossed in butter for a delicious vegetable, or made into a tasty soup. For this recipe it is preferable to use the flesh from a medium-sized pumpkin which will give more flavour.

1kg/2lb pumpkin, peeled
25g/1oz butter
1 tsp grated ginger
¼ tsp turmeric
¼ tsp grated nutmeg
salt & pepper
900ml/1½ pints creamy milk
a little single cream, to serve

Reserve the seeds from the pumpkin. Discard any stringy core and dice the flesh. Melt the butter in a saucepan with a heatproof handle, or a flameproof casserole, and add the pumpkin and ginger. Toss in the butter and then add the spices and seasoning and fry for about 10 minutes, until softening. Add the milk, bring to the boil and then transfer to the simmering oven, covered, for 30 minutes until the pumpkin is soft. Pureé the soup, check the seasoning and re-heat.

Serve the soup topped with a whirl of cream.

Serves 6

PUMPKIN SEEDS

Wash and clean the seeds from a pumpkin and lay them on a baking tray. Put the oven shelf on the second set of runners from the top of the roasting oven and slide in the tray of pumpkin seeds. Roast for a few minutes; watch that they do not burn! Toss in a little coarse salt and serve as drinks nibbles.

LONDON PARTICULAR

London fogs, commonly known as 'pea-soupers,' gave the name to this hearty, warming soup. Use either bacon rashers and chicken stock, or a small bacon knuckle joint and water instead of stock. If the joint is salty, soak it for several hours in clear water.

25g/1oz butter
50g/2oz bacon, rinded & diced
Or 1 small bacon knuckle joint
1 onion, peeled & chopped
1 carrot, peeled & chopped
1 stick of celery, trimmed & chopped
450g/1lb dried split peas, rinsed
2.3l/4 pints chicken stock or water
salt & pepper
croûtons

Melt the butter in a large saucepan with a heatproof handle, or a flameproof casserole, and fry the onion, carrot, celery and bacon, if using, for 5–10 minutes. Stir in the dried split peas, and stock or water and the bacon joint, if using. Cover, bring to the boil and simmer for 5 minutes before moving to the simmering oven for 2 hours.

Remove from the oven and lift out the bacon joint. Remove the meat from the bone, dice and reserve some if you like chunky soup. Purée the soup mixture with the bacon. Adjust the seasoning. Re-heat and serve with croûtons and pieces of reserved bacon.

Serves 8

ROAST GARLIC

I love cloves of garlic roasted with peppers and courgettes. The first time I ever had whole roast garlic was when a French friend served it as a starter for dinner. Somehow, the Aga makes the roast garlic taste even sweeter. Allow one bulb of garlic per person.

4 whole bulbs of garlic
4 tbsp olive oil
salt & pepper

Trim the top off each bulb of garlic to expose the flesh of the centre cloves. Stand in an ovenproof dish and brush each bulb generously with oil. Season with salt and pepper. Roast on the third set of runners from the top of the roasting oven for 20 minutes. The outer skin will be crisp and the cloves soft.

Each person can scoop out their cloves with a teaspoon.

Serve the bulbs with their juices and crusty bread.

Serves 4

MAURITIAN FISH CURRY

I have specified squid here, but this recipe is versatile, so you could use any firm, fleshed fish, such as monkfish or cod. Since the fish is added at the end of the cooking, it's easy to ensure that it is not overcooked.

1 tbsp coriander seeds
1 tsp cumin seeds
2 shallots, finely chopped
2 cloves of garlic
1 tsp finely chopped fresh ginger
1 lemon grass stalk, chopped
20 curry leaves
2 red chillies, seeded & roughly chopped
2 tsp curry powder
1 tsp salt
2 tbsp vegetable oil
225g/8oz tomatoes, skinned & quartered
225ml/8fl oz thick coconut milk
225ml/8fl oz fish stock
450g/1lb squid, cut into bite-size pieces
pepper

Put the coriander seeds and cumin seeds into a dry frying pan and heat on the simmering plate for 3–4 minutes. Tip the seeds into a food processor or blender and add the shallots, garlic, ginger, lemon grass, curry leaves, chillies, curry powder and salt. Blend to a fine paste.

Heat the oil in a saucepan and fry the curry paste for about 5 minutes, taking care not to let it burn. Add the tomatoes and cook for a further 5 minutes, then stir in the coconut milk and stock, cooking and stirring until an oily sheen develops. At this stage the sauce can be set aside to let the flavours mature.

Add the squid to the sauce and bring to the boil. Simmer very gently for about 5 minutes, until the fish is cooked. Taste and adjust the seasoning.

Serve with rice.

Serves 4

COCONUT COD CURRY

If you are lucky enough to have a fishmonger who sells fresh fish, this is a good way to serve cod, or haddock, when the days are beginning to feel a little chilly. If you like hot curry sauces, replace the green chillies with hot red chillies.

5 tbsp vegetable oil
4 cod or haddock steaks
225g/8oz onion, chopped
2 green chillies, seeded & chopped
2.5cm/1 inch piece of fresh ginger, chopped
2 cloves of garlic, crushed
1/2 tsp turmeric
2 tsp curry paste
400ml/14fl oz can of coconut milk
2 tbsp chopped coriander
salt & pepper
3 tbsp lime juice

Heat the oil in a large frying pan and fry the fish steaks for 1–2 minutes on each side, until golden-brown. To prevent smells in the kitchen the frying pan can be placed on the floor of the roasting oven, providing it has a heatproof handle. Remove the fish to a plate.

Fry the onion and chillies until golden-brown. Add the ginger, garlic, turmeric and curry paste. Cook for 1 minute and then stir in the coconut milk and coriander and simmer until thickened and syrupy. Strain through a sieve and return to the rinsed pan. Check the seasoning and add the fish. Simmer gently for a few minutes until the fish is cooked. Add the lime juice and serve immediately.

Serves 4

MOULES MARINIÈRE

Mussels are plentiful and fairly inexpensive. Fresh British mussels are available from September to April. When buying mussels allow about 15 per person, that is about 450g (1lb) or 600ml (1 pint).

1.8kg/4lb mussels
salt & pepper
300ml/1/2 pint fish stock
150ml/1/4 pint white wine
2 shallots, finely chopped
1 clove of garlic, crushed
2 celery sticks, chopped
150ml/1/4 pint double cream
1 tbsp lemon juice
1 tbsp chopped parsley

Wash and scrub the mussels well. Place in clean water with a little salt for 1 hour to help remove any sand. Remove and throw away any mussels that are broken or that do not close when tapped. Drain the water from the sound mussels and place them in a large, wide-bottomed pan. Add the fish stock, wine, shallots, garlic and celery. Bring to the boil and simmer for 3–4 minutes, until the mussels open. Any mussels that are still closed should be thrown away.

Strain the liquor through a sieve into a clean pan and bring to the boil until reduced. Stir in the cream, salt and pepper, lemon juice and parsley. Arrange the mussels in serving dishes and pour over the creamy liquor.

Serve immediately with good French bread.

Serves 4

SKATE WITH BLACK BUTTER

Skate wings are frequently seen on fish counters or stalls in the autumn. The ammonia smell and the slimy skin disappear on cooking. After cooking, the bones are easy to remove.

1.8kgs/4lb skate wings
2 shallots, finely diced
1.25l/2 pints fish stock
50g/2oz capers
juice of 1 lemon
100g/4oz butter
1 tbsp white wine vinegar
2 tbsp chopped parsley

Wash the skate wings well and lay in the large roasting tin. Sprinkle with the shallots and then add the fish stock. Hang the roasting tin on the third set of runners from the top of the roasting oven for 15–20 minutes until the main bones lift from the flesh. Carefully remove the bones and place the fish on a serving plate. Sprinkle with the capers.

Melt the butter in a pan and cook until nut-brown and foaming. Add the lemon juice, vinegar and parsley and pour over the fish.

Serve immediately with buttered potatoes and a green vegetable.

Serves 8

ROAST PORK WITH APPLES

I often cook this roast for cookery demonstrations because it shows potential Aga owners how good roast meat tastes when cooked in an Aga. Cooking apples this way saves having to make apple sauce.

1 lemon, halved
1.6kg/3½ lb loin of pork
salt & pepper
6 Cox's apples, quartered & cored
1 tbsp flour
150ml/¼ pint white wine
150ml/¼ pint chicken stock

Rub the pork skin well with the cut surfaces of the lemon. Stand the pork in the small roasting tin and hang on the second set of runners from the top of the roasting oven for 30 minutes per 450g/1lb plus 30 minutes extra.

Season the apple quarters and add to the roasting tin for the last 20 minutes of the cooking time.

Remove the meat and apples to a warm serving plate and drain off any excess fat from the roasting tin. Stand the roasting tin on the simmering plate and whisk in the flour. When smooth, whisk in the wine and stock and allow to bubble well until thickened.

Serve the sauce with the roast pork and apple slices.

Serves 6–8

ROAST GAMMON WITH PLUMS AND REDCURRANT GLAZE

I love gammon. It is easy to cook and left-overs can be eaten in so many ways. My husband likes a gammon joint not only for the flavour but because it is easy to carve! This recipe works well with autumn plums.

1 gammon joint, about 1.25kg/3lb
2 tbsp redcurrant jelly
1 tbsp mustard
2 tbsp golden syrup
1/4 tsp allspice
pepper
8 plums, halved & stones removed

Place the gammon in the small roasting tin and cover loosely with foil. Slide onto the bottom set of runners of the roasting oven for 30 minutes per 450g/1lb plus 30 minutes extra.

In a small basin, place the redcurrant jelly, mustard, golden syrup, allspice and a grinding of pepper. Stand the basin on the back of the Aga and leave the mixture to melt while the gammon is roasting. Stir to mix when melted to make the glaze.

Thirty minutes before the end of the cooking time, remove the foil from the meat. With a sharp knife, cut the skin from the gammon. Spoon over the glaze and arrange the plums around the base of the joint. Return to the oven and cook for the remaining 30 minutes.

Slice the gammon and serve with the plums.

Serves 8

RATATOUILLE WITH AIR-DRIED HAM

The addition of the air-dried ham at the end of cooking turns ratatouille into a lovely main course. If you like, some vinaigrette can be poured over before serving, but I think the vegetables are moist enough. The vegetables below are only suggestions and you can use what you have to hand or what is plentiful.

2 courgettes, cut into 2.5cm/1 inch cubes
1 aubergine, cut into 2.5cm/1 inch cubes
1 red pepper, halved & seeded, cut into 2.5cm/1 inch cubes
1 yellow pepper, halved & seeded, cut into 2.5cm/1 inch cubes
1 red onion, quartered
2 cloves of garlic
450g/1lb tomatoes, quartered
3 tbsp olive oil
salt
100g/4oz air-dried ham

Put the vegetables in the small roasting tin, drizzle over the oil and season with salt. Hang the roasting tin on the top set of runners of the roasting oven and cook the vegetables for about 40 minutes, until tender and tinged brown.

Just before serving, tear the air-dried ham into pieces and add to the vegetables.

Serves 4

RABBIT AND WILD MUSHROOM CASSEROLE

The best rabbit meat is found in the autumn and many types of wild mushroom are also available at this time. Some people are a little sentimental about eating rabbit, but it is a cheap, flavoursome meat. This is a perfect dish for cooking in the Aga when the days are getting cooler and darker. Serve with creamy mashed potatoes to soak up the delicious sauce.

1 rabbit, jointed
2 tbsp seasoned flour
25g/1oz butter
1 tbsp vegetable oil
2 large onions, quartered & sliced
175g/6oz mushrooms, sliced
150ml/1/4 pint white wine
300ml/1/2 pint chicken stock
salt & pepper
4 bay leaves
3 tbsp crème fraîche

Toss the rabbit joints in seasoned flour. This is easiest to do if you put the flour, salt and pepper in a plastic bag, add the rabbit, hold the bag closed and shake it well. The meat should be evenly coated.

Melt the butter and heat the oil in a flameproof casserole. Brown the rabbit in batches, and then move to a plate. When all the meat has browned add the onions to the residue in the pan and stir well. Return the rabbit to the casserole and add the mushrooms. Pour on the wine, bubble the mixture for 1–2 minutes and then add the stock, salt and pepper and bay leaves. Cover, bring to the boil and then transfer to the simmering oven for 3–4 hours.

Stir in the crème fraîche just before serving.

Serves 4

DUCK BREASTS WITH BLACKBERRY SAUCE

I love picking blackberries. I usually have the children for company and it seems such an idyllic way to spend a warm September afternoon, gathering food for free with chance of a peaceful chat. The problem with taking the children is that, although they are not fearful of the brambles, they usually eat most of the berries they pick!

4 duck breasts
2 tbsp honey
salt & pepper
225g/8oz blackberries
4 tbsp water
1 tbsp lemon juice
2 tsp sugar, or to taste
1 tsp cornflour,
blended with a little water

Score the skin of the duck breasts by making 4–5 diagonal cuts. Place on a rack in the small roasting tin, skin side uppermost. Mix the honey and salt and pepper together and brush over the duck breasts. Slide the tin onto the second set of runners from the top of the roasting oven and grill the duck for 20–25 minutes.

Reserve a few blackberries for garnishing and place the remaining berries, the water, lemon juice and sugar in a saucepan and bring slowly to the boil. Simmer for about 5 minutes, crushing the fruit to release the juices. Pass the sauce through a sieve and return to the rinsed saucepan. Stir in the slaked cornflour and bring to the boil to thicken the sauce.

Slice the duck breasts and lay on serving plates. Add the blackberry sauce, and a few blackberries, to garnish.

Serves 4

ROAST DUCK WITH REDCURRANT GLAZE

Duck has become a fashionable meat, but duck breasts are favoured because they are easy to cook and serve. I prefer a whole roast duck for the fullest flavour, even though serving is not as elegant.

1 duck, about 2.5kg/4¾lb
100g/4oz redcurrant jelly
1 orange, the zest removed with a zester & the juice squeezed
1 tbsp juniper berries, crushed
salt & pepper
orange wedges, to garnish (optional)

Remove any giblets and excess fat from inside the bird. Prick the skin of the duck all over and then stand on the rack set inside the small roasting tin. Hang the tin on the third set of runners from the top of the roasting oven for 20 minutes per 450g/1lb plus 20 minutes extra.

Put the redcurrant jelly, orange zest and juice, juniper berries and salt and pepper in a basin at the back of the Aga and leave the jelly to soften, then mix together well.

Twenty minutes before the end of cooking time, spoon half the redcurrant glaze over the duck. Return to the oven. When the duck is cooked transfer to a warm serving plate and leave to 'rest' for 10 minutes before serving.

Pour the excess fat from the roasting tin and then stand the tin on the simmering plate. Pour in the remaining glaze and heat through for 1–2 minutes. Pour the hot glaze over the duck and serve garnished with orange wedges, if liked.

Serves 4

ROAST PHEASANT WITH ONION CONFITURE

Onion confiture is delicious served hot or cold with any cold meat as well as roast pork and roast pheasant. The confiture takes a while to cook so I recommend making it the day before you need it. Any left-over confiture will keep well in the fridge.

75g/3oz butter, plus extra for smearing
700g/1½lb onions, chopped
175g/6oz sugar
salt & pepper
100ml/4fl oz red wine vinegar
225ml/8fl oz red wine
2 tbsp crème de cassis
1 pheasant

In a wide saucepan with a heatproof handle, heat the butter and stir in the onions, sugar and plenty of salt and pepper. Cover the pan and leave on the simmering plate for about 5 minutes and then transfer to the simmering oven for 1 hour. Remove from the oven to the simmering plate and add the vinegar, wine and crème de cassis. Stir well and bring to the boil. Take off the lid and return the saucepan to the simmering oven for 2–3 hours. The mixture should be the consistency of jam; if necessary simmer on the simmering plate to finally thicken for a few minutes.

Place the pheasant in the small roasting tin and smear well with butter and salt and pepper. Hang the tin on the third set of runners from the top of the roasting oven and roast for about 45 minutes, until brown and the juices from inside the legs run clear.

Serve with the warmed onion confiture.

Serves 4

ROAST PARTRIDGE
WITH APRICOT STUFFING

It is now possible to buy partridge in supermarkets as well as from game dealers. Should you not be able to find partridge, you can use poussins instead.

8 rashers of streaky bacon
4 young partridges
225g/8oz pork sausagemeat
50g/2oz dried apricots, diced
2 tbsp chopped parsley
salt & pepper
1 tbsp flour
300ml/½ pint chicken stock

Wrap 2 bacon rashers in a cross over the breasts of the partridge. Put the partridge in the small roasting tin and hang the tin on the third set of runners from the top of the roasting oven and roast for 40 minutes.

Mix the sausagemeat, apricots, parsley and salt and pepper with your hands and then form into 8 even-sized balls.

After 10 minutes of roasting, place the stuffing balls round the partridges. At the end of cooking time the birds should have a golden skin and any juices from the insides of the legs should run clear.

Place the partridges on a warm serving plate with the stuffing balls. Stand the roasting tin on the simmering plate. Using a wire whisk, stir in the flour and allow to thicken before slowly adding the stock to make a smooth gravy. Adjust the seasoning and serve with the partridge.

Serves 4

HARE AND WHISKY CASSEROLE

Use this recipe for older hares; young ones are best roasted and served with a creamy sauce or a fresh blackcurrant sauce. Rabbit or venison can be substituted for the hare.

1 hare, jointed
4 small onions, chopped
4 sticks of celery, roughly chopped
salt & pepper
25g/1oz seasoned flour
75g/3oz streaky bacon, diced
50g/2oz butter
1/2 tsp dried mixed herbs
1/2 tsp ground cloves
150ml/1/4 pint whisky

Choose the meatiest joints and set aside. Place the remaining joints in a saucepan with a heatproof handle, or a flameproof casserole, and add a little of the onion and celery and salt and pepper. Cover with water and a lid and bring to the boil. Transfer to the simmering oven for 2 hours to make a good stock. Strain off and reserve the stock.

Toss the reserved meaty joints in seasoned flour. Fry the bacon in a frying pan until the fat runs, and then brown the hare joints. Transfer to a casserole. Fry the remaining onions and celery and the herbs and cloves until softening and just tinging with colour. Add the whisky and 600ml/1 pint of hare stock. Bring to the boil and pour into the casserole. Return to the boil and transfer to the simmering oven for 3 hours, until the meat is tender. Serve with baked or mashed potatoes.

Serves 6–8

BRAISED BEEF WITH CHESTNUTS

This is a dish to make in the autumn when chestnuts are in season. Chestnuts can be terrible to prepare, but they do add a special flavour to the casserole.

18 fresh chestnuts
1kg/2lb stewing beef, cubed
1 tbsp seasoned flour
25g/1oz butter
1 tbsp vegetable oil
1 onion, chopped
150ml/1/4 pint beef stock
300ml/1/2 pint brown ale
grated nutmeg
finely grated rind & juice of 1 orange
salt & pepper
chopped parsley

Slit the skins of the chestnuts and place in a saucepan. Cover with water and simmer for 7 minutes. Drain and while still warm, peel off the thick outer skin and the thin inner skin.

Toss the meat in the seasoned flour. Heat the butter and oil in a large frying pan and brown the meat in batches. Drain and transfer to a flameproof casserole. Add the onion to the pan and cook until softening. Add to the meat. Stir the stock and beer into the frying pan and bring to the boil. Add a seasoning of nutmeg, the orange juice and salt and pepper. Pour over the meat. Stir in the chestnuts. Place the casserole either on the simmering plate or on the floor of the roasting oven and bring to the boil.

Transfer to the simmering oven and cook for 2–3 hours, until the meat is tender. Stir in the orange rind and sprinkle with chopped parsley to serve.

Serves 6

STOVED CHICKEN

A traditional Scottish recipe for a warming chicken dish that will not spoil in the simmering oven. Choose a floury variety of potato such as King Edward.

50g/2oz butter
4 chicken quarters, halved
100g/4oz lean back bacon, rind removed & chopped
1kg/2lb potatoes, sliced
2 onions, sliced
salt & pepper
2 tsp thyme, chopped
450ml/3/4 pint chicken stock

Heat the butter in a frying pan and fry the chicken and bacon until golden-brown.

Place a good layer of potatoes and onions in the base of a casserole. Season well and sprinkle over some of the thyme. Add the chicken and bacon followed by another layer of onion, potato and thyme. Pour over the stock and then any butter remaining in the pan. Season the top of the potatoes. Cover.

Put the casserole on the floor of the roasting oven for 15–20 minutes, until piping hot and then transfer to the simmering oven for 2–3 hours. Serve with a fresh green vegetable.

Serves 4

ORIENTAL TURKEY ESCALOPES WITH PLUMS

Autumn plums work so well in this slightly oriental dish. Damsons make a wonderful alternative to plums if you can get them. Allow time for the turkey to marinate overnight to tenderise the flesh and add flavour. Chicken can be substituted for turkey.

2 turkey breast fillets, skinned
75ml/3fl oz apple juice
3 tbsp soy sauce
3 tbsp dry sherry
1 clove of garlic, crushed
1 tsp sugar
1 tsp chopped thyme
1 tbsp vegetable oil
225g/8oz plums,
halved & stones removed

Cut each turkey breast in half. Flatten lightly with a rolling pin and then cut each portion into 2 pieces. Place in a shallow non-metallic, dish and pour over the apple juice, soy sauce, sherry, garlic, sugar and thyme. Cover and leave in a cool place overnight, or for 3–4 hours.

Heat the oil in a frying pan with a heatproof handle. Drain the turkey from the marinade; reserve the marinade. Fry the turkey on both sides and then add the plums and reserved marinade. Cover. Place the shelf on the floor of the roasting oven and slide in the turkey pan. Cook for 15–20 minutes, until tender.

Serves 4

SPINACH GNOCCHI

Fresh spinach has a long season in this country, so this dish can be made in the spring or summer, but I like to serve it as an autumn supper dish, when the slightly older leaves have a stronger flavour. The recipe can also be served in smaller quantities as a starter.

450g/1lb fresh spinach, thick stalks removed & well washed
175g/6oz Ricotta cheese
50g/2oz flour
1 egg yolk
50g/2oz Gruyère cheese, grated
salt & pepper,
grated nutmeg

Sauce:
15g/¹/₂oz butter
15g/¹/₂oz flour
450ml/³/₄ pint milk
50g/2oz Gruyère cheese, grated
pepper

Place the spinach in a saucepan with a lid, put on the simmering plate and cook until the spinach has wilted. Drain off any excess moisture and chop the spinach very finely or purée in a food processor or blender.

Mix the spinach with the Ricotta cheese and flour. Then beat in the egg yolk, Gruyère cheese, a little salt and pepper and a grating of nutmeg.

Dust your hands with flour and shape teaspoonfuls of mixture into little balls. Chill well.

Place a large pan of salted water on the boiling plate to boil.

Meanwhile, make the sauce: place the butter, flour and milk into a saucepan and whisk on the simmering plate until boiling and thickened. Remove from the heat and stir in the cheese and pepper. Keep warm while cooking the gnocchi.

Drop the gnocchi, one at a time, into the pan of boiling water. When they float to the surface the gnocchi are ready. Remove with a slotted spoon and place in a shallow ovenproof dish. Pour over the sauce and grate over a little nutmeg.

Serves 4

POTATO CAKES

Potato cakes are good served with bacon, chops and poached fish. I sometimes make a large potato cake and sprinkle some Double Gloucester cheese over the top for a supper dish. Serve with a salad for a complete meal. This potato cake recipe is a cross between a cake and a rösti. It is really best to use a food processor, but if you don't have one, use a grater for the potatoes.

450g/1lb main crop potatoes
1 small onion
salt & pepper
1 egg
2 tbsp flour
1 tbsp chopped parsley
1 tbsp oil

Place the potatoes and onion in the food processor and whizz to roughly chop the vegetables. Add the salt and pepper, egg and flour and whizz once more to mix. Allow to stand for 10 minutes. Mix the parsley into the potato mixture and shape into flat cake shapes. Heat the oil in a frying pan and fry the cakes for 5 minutes on each side, until cooked through.

Makes 6

MUSHROOM TARTS

These tarts make a tasty lunch or supper dish for mushroom lovers. If you have wild mushrooms you can leave out the Worcestershire sauce, because the mushrooms will have enough flavour.

225g/8oz shortcrust pastry
25g/1oz butter
225g/8oz assorted mushrooms, diced
1 tbsp Worcestershire sauce
2 eggs
300ml/1/2 pint single cream
salt & pepper

Roll out the pastry and line 4 individual tart tins. Chill.

Melt the butter in a saucepan and fry the mushrooms. Season with the Worcestershire sauce. Cool, then scatter over the base of the pastry cases. Beat together the eggs, cream and salt and pepper. Pour over the mushrooms. Bake the tarts on the floor of the roasting oven for 15 minutes, until the custard is just set and the pastry golden.

Serves 4

WARM RED CABBAGE SALAD

Make this salad version of the red cabbage and apple theme in autumn when fresh apples and walnuts are available. If I serve this dish on its own, I add rolls of air-dried ham.

20 walnut halves
2 tbsp walnut oil
1 clove of garlic, finely chopped
2 tbsp balsamic vinegar
1 small red onion, finely sliced
1 small red cabbage, shredded
salt & pepper
1 eating apple, cored & sliced
100g/4oz goats' cheese, broken into bite-size pieces
1 tbsp chopped parsley

Place the walnuts in a small ovenproof dish and sprinkle on about 2 teaspoons of walnut oil. Put towards the top of the roasting oven and toast the nuts for 5–7 minutes. Keep an eye on the nuts so that they don't burn! Remove and cool.

Put the garlic, vinegar and remaining walnut oil in a large, shallow pan on the simmering plate. When it is hot, add the onion, stir and then add the cabbage, stirring well for about 2 minutes. Season with salt and pepper. Remove from the heat and add the walnuts, apple, goats' cheese and parsley. Toss and serve.

Serves 4–6

VEGETARIAN STUFFED MARROW

So many times in the autumn I am given a marrow, usually by people who like growing them but don't quite know what to do with them. I often make marrow and ginger jam, or this vegetarian savoury dish.

25g/1oz butter
700g/1½lb marrow, peeled & halved lengthways & seeds removed
2 parsnips, diced
2 carrots, diced
100g/4oz swede, diced
100g/4oz turnip, diced
1 tbsp chopped parsley
1 generous tbsp tomato purée
scant 150ml/¼ pint vegetable stock
salt & pepper

Melt the butter in a saucepan and fry the vegetables for 5–10 minutes. Add the parsley, tomato purée, and stock, cover, bring to the boil and transfer to the simmering oven for 20–25 minutes.

Stand half the marrow on a baking tray and fill the cavity with the vegetable filling. Cover with the second marrow half. Wrap in foil.

Bake on the second set of runners from the bottom of the roasting oven for 40–45 minutes. Serve hot, cut into slices.

Serves 4

COFFEE AND WALNUT ROULADE

Fresh English walnuts become available in early autumn, so if you should be lucky enough to have a walnut tree that fruits well, use the fresh nuts for this recipe. Alternatively, some markets are a good source of nuts in the autumn.

5 eggs, separated
150g/5oz caster sugar
3 tbsp self-raising flour
2 tsp coffee granules, blended
with 2 tbsp boiling water
icing sugar, for dusting

Filling:
100g/4oz walnuts, roughly chopped
300ml/1/2 pint whipping cream, whipped

Line the large roasting tin with a sheet of either re-usable baking paper or oiled greaseproof paper.

Place the egg yolks and the sugar into a basin and whisk until light and fluffy. Fold in the flour and coffee. Whisk the egg whites until stiff. Beat 1 tablespoon of egg white into the coffee mixture and then carefully fold in the remaining egg white. Spread the mixture into the lined tin.

For a two oven Aga: put the roasting tin on the bottom set of runners of the roasting oven and slide in the cold shelf on the third set of runners from the bottom for 15–20 minutes, until the roulade is firm to the touch and golden-brown.

For a four oven Aga: put the roasting tin on the second set of runners from the bottom of the baking oven and bake the roulade for 15–20 minutes, until firm to the touch and golden-brown.

Remove the roulade from the oven and cover the top with either a plain sheet of re-usable baking paper or a clean tea-towel. Leave until cold.

Tip the roulade onto the sheet of baking paper or greaseproof paper. Remove the tin-lining sheet and spread the roulade with whipped cream. Scatter over the nuts. Roll up lengthwise and put on a serving plate with the join at the bottom. Dust with icing sugar.

Serves 8

PEAR AND CURD CHEESE TART

New season pears are around in the autumn when their fresh taste can be enjoyed raw or lightly poached with a cinnamon stick. The pears for this recipe need to be ripe and not hard. Finish the meringue topping just before serving otherwise it will go soggy.

Sweet shortcrust pastry:
225g/8oz plain flour
50g/2oz caster sugar
salt
100g/4oz butter, diced
1 egg, beaten

Filling:
4 pears, peeled, cored & cut into 8 slices
200g/7oz cream cheese
2 egg yolks
1 tsp vanilla essence
50g/2oz caster sugar
1 tbsp lemon juice
1 tbsp vegetable oil
3 tbsp milk

Meringue topping:
2 egg whites
50g/2oz icing sugar

Make the pastry: put the flour, sugar and salt into a mixing bowl. Add the butter, and rub in until the mixture resembles breadcrumbs. Add the egg and enough cold water to make a firm, pliable dough. Wrap and set aside to rest.

Roll out the pastry and line a 23cm/9 inch loose-based flan tin.

Make the filling: lay the pear slices in the pastry case, fanning round from the centre. Beat together the cream cheese, egg yolks, vanilla essence, caster sugar, lemon juice, oil and milk. Spread over the pears.

Bake the tart on the floor of the roasting oven, with the cold shelf on the second set of runners from the bottom, for 20–30 minutes, until set.

Make the topping: whisk the egg whites and icing sugar until stiff, and spread over the pears. Return to the oven for a further 10 minutes, until the top is pale-gold.

Serves 6–8

APPLE AND MINCEMEAT FILO TART

Although this tart contains mincemeat, which is usually associated with Christmas-time, I feel that this is a good pudding to make when there is a glut of apples in autumn or early winter. Use a loose-bottomed or spring-release tin so the tart can be turned out for serving. Cooking the tart on the floor of the Aga means that the pastry base will be crisp despite the fruit filling.

1kg/2lb eating apples, peeled, cored & roughly chopped
450g/1lb jar of mincemeat
75g/3oz butter, melted
8–10 sheets of filo pastry
icing sugar, for dusting

Place the apples in a saucepan with 1–2 tablespoons of water and heat gently on the simmering plate until just softening. Stir in the mincemeat and set aside off the heat.

Brush the base and side of a 23cm/9 inch loose-bottomed or spring-release cake tin with some of the melted butter. Brush the sheets of filo pastry with most of the remaining butter and use to line the tin. Leave the filo pastry sheets overlapping the edge of the tin. Pour in the apple and mincemeat mixture and fold over the filo pastry. Leave a circle in the middle so that the filling can be seen, and wrinkle up the pastry topping a little. Brush on the remaining butter.

Bake on the floor of the roasting oven for 20–25 minutes. Slide in the cold shelf on the second set of runners from the bottom, if the pastry is browning too much on top.

Dust with icing sugar and serve warm.

Serves 6–8

PLUM AND ALMOND TART

The plum is a wonderful and versatile autumnal fruit that is perfect next to ham or pork and equally fine for puddings, jams and chutneys.

225g/8oz plain flour
2 tbsp caster sugar
100g/4oz butter, diced
salt
1 egg, beaten
2 tbsp apricot jam
1 tbsp water
Filling:
75g/3oz butter, softened
75g/3oz caster sugar
1 egg, beaten
50g/2oz ground almonds
1 tbsp plain flour
225g/8oz firm plums, halved & stones removed
25g/1oz blanched almonds

Put the flour, sugar, salt and butter in a mixing bowl and rub in the butter until the mixture looks like fresh breadcrumbs. Add the egg and enough water to make a firm dough. Roll the pastry to fit a 23cm (9 inch) flan tin or dish. Chill well.

Place the jam and water in a small basin and stand on the back of the Aga to soften.

Make the filling: cream together the butter and sugar. When light and fluffy, beat in the egg and then the ground almonds and flour. Spread in the pastry case. Place the plums on top, cut side upper-most. Scatter over the blanched almonds.

Bake on the floor of the roasting oven for 25–30 minutes, until the pastry is golden-brown and the plums softening. Glaze with the warmed jam mixture.

Serves 6–8

APRICOT AND BANANA TART

Fresh apricots have a short season. Really ripe apricots are delicious eaten raw, but cooking can enhance the flavour of under-ripe fruit. Bananas add sweetness to this tart without masking the flavour of the apricots.

225g/8oz sweet shortcrust pastry
225g/8oz mascarpone cheese
2 eggs, beaten
2–3 drops vanilla essence
25g/1oz caster sugar
450g/1lb fresh apricots, halved & stones removed
2 bananas, sliced
4 tbsp apricot jam, warmed on top of the Aga to soften

Roll out the pastry and line either a loose-bottomed 33 x 10cm /13 x 4 inch tranche tin or a 23cm/9 inch round flan tin. Chill.

Beat together the mascarpone cheese, eggs, vanilla essence and caster sugar. Lay the bananas over the base of the pastry case and then cover with the apricot halves. Pour over the mascarpone mixture. Tap the tin on the work surface to settle the filling.

Bake on the floor of the roasting oven for 30–40 minutes, until the filling is set and the pastry is golden-brown.

Brush the top with apricot jam to glaze before serving.

Serves 6-8

APRICOT AND ALMOND TART

A useful way to make a few precious apricots go further. The flavours of apricots and almonds marry well together.

225g/8oz shortcrust pastry
1 egg, separated
450g/1lb fresh apricots, halved & stones removed
50g/2oz butter, softened
50g/2oz caster sugar
50g/2oz ground almonds
1 egg, beaten
25g/1oz flaked almonds

Roll out the pastry and use to line a shallow 23cm/9 inch flan tin. Brush the pastry base with the egg yolk.

Lay the apricots over the pastry base, cut side down.

Cream together the butter and sugar. Beat in the ground almonds and then the whole beaten egg. Whisk the remaining egg white and fold into the creamed mixture. Spread over the apricots and scatter on the flaked almonds.

Bake on the floor of the roasting oven for 20–25 minutes, until the pastry is crisp and golden-brown and the filling is set. If the top is browning too quickly slide the cold shelf in two runners above for the last 5 minutes.

Serves 6–8

APPLE AND HAZELNUT BISCUIT

The combination of apples and hazelnuts make such a wonderful autumnal dish that it has been a favourite pudding for many years. The two parts can be made in advance but assemble the pudding no more than 15 minutes before the meal starts otherwise the apple will make the biscuit soft.

75g/3oz butter
3 tbsp caster sugar
100g/4oz plain flour
salt
75g/3oz ground or chopped hazelnuts
icing sugar, for dusting

Filling:
450g/1lb eating apples, peeled, cored & sliced
grated rind of 1 lemon
1 tbsp apricot jam
1 tbsp sultanas

Cream the butter and sugar then stir in the flour, salt and nuts. Knead together to make a firm dough. Cut the dough in half and pat out to circles about 20cm/8 inches in diameter, onto 2 baking trays.

For a two-oven Aga, put the oven shelf on the floor of the roasting oven and slide in the baking tray. Put the cold shelf on the second set of runners from the bottom and bake the biscuits for 10–15 minutes, until pale-golden-brown.

For a four-oven Aga, place the shelf on the second set of runners from the bottom of the baking oven and bake the biscuits for 10–15 minutes, until pale-golden-brown.

Cut one of the circles into 8 triangles while warm. Leave to cool.

Make the filling: put the apples in a saucepan with the lemon rind and jam. Cook over a gentle heat until the apples are soft but still holding their shape. This may take only a few minutes depending upon the type of apples. Stir in the sultanas.

Just before serving, place the complete biscuit circle on a plate, cover with the apple mixture and arrange the triangles on top. Dust with icing sugar.

Serves 8

BLUEBERRY PANCAKES

Blueberries are often thought of as exclusively American, but they are grown in this country and crop from July to October. Blackcurrants can be substituted in this recipe, and give a similar sharp flavour. Make the pancakes either on the simmering plate or in a lightly greased frying pan on the boiling plate.

150g/5oz plain flour
225ml/8fl oz milk
1 tsp vanilla sugar
1 tbsp melted butter
salt
3 eggs, separated
1 tsp caster sugar
225g/8 oz blueberries
4 tsp caster sugar mixed
with 1 tsp cinnamon
oil, for greasing

Place the flour in a mixing bowl and whisk in the milk, vanilla sugar, butter, salt and egg yolks to make a smooth batter. Whisk the egg whites with the caster sugar until stiff and then fold into the batter.

Oil the simmering plate lightly and ladle half the batter into 2 portions on the oiled plate to make pancakes about 2 cm/3/4 inch thick. Sprinkle a quarter of the blueberries over each pancake and allow the batter to set. Carefully turn over and brown for 1–2 minutes.

Continue to cook the remaining 2 pancakes. Serve on individual plates and dust with the cinnamon sugar.

Serves 4

CARROT BREAD

An adapted American carrot loaf recipe that helped rid me of some end-of-season, flavourless carrots. It is excellent spread with soft cream cheese and a variety of toppings such as glacé icing and glacé fruit.

225g/8oz soft butter or margarine
100g/4oz caster sugar
100g/4oz soft brown sugar
225g/8oz plain flour
1 tsp baking powder
1 tsp bicarbonate of soda
1 tsp salt
1 tsp ground cinnamon
75g/3oz walnuts, chopped
3 eggs
250g/9oz carrots, grated

Line a 1kg/2lb loaf tin. Cream the butter and sugars. Mix together the flour, baking powder, bicarbonate of soda, salt, cinnamon and walnuts. Gradually beat the eggs into the creamed mixture, adding a little flour with each addition. Fold in the remaining flour mixture, and then the carrots. Spoon into the tin.

For a two-oven Aga, stand the loaf tin in the large roasting tin and hang on the bottom set of runners of the roasting oven. Slide the cold shelf onto the third set of runners from the top of the oven. Bake for approximately 50 minutes, until golden-brown and shrunk from the sides of the tin and a skewer inserted into the middle comes out clean.

For a four-oven Aga, slide the shelf onto the second set of runners from the bottom of the baking oven and bake the loaf for 50–60 minutes, until the loaf is golden-brown and shrunk from the sides of the tin and a skewer inserted into the middle comes out clean. Cool the loaf in the tin for about 10 minutes and then turn out onto a cooling rack until cold.

Cuts into 10–12 slices

DRIED PLUMS

Plum trees have a habit of giving you a bumper crop one year and a lean crop the next. If you have a bumper crop, this is one way of preserving some of the plums and their flavour for the winter. The same method can be used for other stone fruits.

ripe fruits, such as plums & greengages, stones removed

Stand the rack inside the large roasting tin. Lay the fruit on the rack, cut side uppermost. Slide the tin onto the middle set of runners of the simmering oven. Dry out for 4–5 hours, until the fruit is about half its original size.

Cool completely before storing. Fruit that is semi-dried can be used as nibbles and in cakes and biscuits. If you increase the drying time so that the fruit is much harder, it will keep longer and can then be used in rich fruit cakes.

CARAMELISED AUTUMN FRUITS

This quick and easy recipe makes a change from poached or stewed fruit. I like it served with ice-cream.

plums, stoned & quartered
pears, peeled, quartered & cored
apples, cored & sliced
demerara sugar

Line a roasting tin with re-usable baking paper or foil. Lay the fruit in a single layer in the tin and scatter with sugar. Hang the tin on the very top runner of the roasting oven and cook for about 15–20 minutes, until the fruit is caramelising and just soft.

BAKED QUINCE WITH
SAFFRON & CLOTTED CREAM

At one time quinces were only available if you grew your own, but now I see them in my local supermarket in the autumn. The cooking time will vary according to the ripeness of the fruit.

4 quinces
pinch of saffron
3 tbsp caster sugar
2–3 tbsp hot water
25g/1oz butter
chilled clotted cream, to serve

Wipe the fluffy skin of the quinces with a damp cloth and cut the fruit in half lengthways. Discard the cores and stand in a shallow ovenproof dish, cut side uppermost. Mix the saffron, 1 teaspoon of sugar and the hot water together. Pour over the quinces.

Sprinkle over the remaining sugar and dot with butter.

Place the oven shelf on the second set of runners from the bottom of the roasting oven and bake the quinces for 35–45 minutes.

Serve warm with chilled clotted cream.

Serves 4

WINTER

ROOT VEGETABLE SOUP

Root vegetables make a sustaining warming family soup. A little cream and chopped parsley stirred in at the end add to the flavour as well as the appearance.

25g/1oz butter
1 large potato, diced
1 large sweet potato, diced
2 carrots, diced
2 parsnips, diced
1 leek, sliced
900ml/1½ pints vegetable or chicken stock
salt & pepper
single cream, to serve
chopped parsley, to garnish

Melt the butter in a roomy saucepan with as heatproof handle, or flameproof casserole, and add the vegetables. Toss well in the butter and fry for a few minutes on the simmering plate. Add the stock and a little salt and pepper. Cover and bring to the boil. Transfer to the simmering oven for 45–60 minutes, until the vegetables are tender. Purée the mixture until smooth. Re-heat and check the seasoning. Serve with a swirl of cream and a sprinkling of parsley.

Serves 4–5

PARSNIP AND APPLE SOUP

Sharp cooking apples compliment the parsnip in this creamy, warming soup for the middle of winter.

25g/1oz butter
700g/1½ lbs parsnips, chopped
1 large cooking apple, peeled, cored & chopped
1.25l/2 pints chicken or vegetable stock
4 sage leaves
150ml/¼ pint single cream
salt & pepper
a few small sage leaves, to garnish

Melt the butter in a roomy saucepan with a heatproof handle, or a flameproof casserole, and fry the parsnips for 1–2 minutes. Then add the apple, cover and cook gently for 5–6 minutes. Add the stock, sage leaves and salt and pepper. Cover and bring to the boil. Transfer to the simmering oven for 30–40 minutes, until the parsnips are cooked. Remove the sage leaves and purée the mixture. Stir in the cream and check the seasoning. Warm through and serve garnished with sage leaves.

Serves 6–8

LEEK, POTATO AND WATERCRESS SOUP

Leek and potato soup is one of my favourites, but when finding a bunch of beautiful fresh watercress in my vegetable box, along with leeks and potatoes, I thought watercress would add a fresh taste. It proved a great hit with the family.

50g/2oz butter
2 large potatoes, roughly diced
3 leeks, sliced
1.25l/2 pints vegetable or chicken stock
1 bunch of watercress, roughly chopped

Melt the butter in a roomy saucepan with a heatproof handle, or a flameproof casserole. Toss the potatoes and leeks in the butter. Cook over a gentle heat, with the pan lid on, for about 5 minutes, but do not brown. Stir in the stock and bring to the boil. Cover and move to the simmering oven for about 45 minutes, until the vegetables are soft. Return to the simmering plate and add the watercress. Cook for 5 minutes and no more otherwise the watercress will lose its colour and flavour.

Purée the soup and check the seasoning. Warm through and serve with a little cream if liked.

Serves 6

TURKEY AND HAZELNUT SOUP

If you are stuck for interesting ideas to use up the turkey at Christmas, do try this soup. Strip the bird of meat and make stock from the carcase.

75g/3oz hazelnuts
25g/1oz butter
1 onion, finely chopped
1/2 tsp paprika
225g/8oz cooked turkey meat, diced
1.25l/2 pints turkey stock
1 egg yolk
150ml/1/4 pint single cream
1 tbsp chopped parsley or chervil
salt & pepper

Put the hazelnuts on a baking tray and place towards the top of the roasting oven for 2–3 minutes until browned. Watch! They burn easily. Cool for 1–2 minutes and then coarsely chop in a food processor.

Heat the butter in a roomy saucepan and fry the onion and paprika until soft but not brown. Add the stock and bring to the boil, then add the turkey meat and simmer for 3–4 minutes, until hot.

Purée the soup in a food processor and return to the rinsed pan. Blend the egg yolk and cream and add to the soup. Heat gently but do not boil. Add the hazelnuts and herbs and adjust the seasoning.

Serves 6

CHEESE CRISPS

I often make these in advance for drinks parties at Christmas. They are fun and simple to make and can be stored for a few days in an airtight container in the fridge. A sheet of re-usable baking paper on the cold shelf will make baking easy.

50g/2oz Cheddar cheese, grated
2 tbsp Parmesan cheese, finely grated

Mix the cheeses together and place small mounds of the mixture on the lined baking tray, allowing space between the mounds for spreading. Flatten with the back of a teaspoon. Slide the tray onto the second set of runners from the top of the roasting oven and bake for 3–4 minutes, until golden round the edges. Transfer to a wire rack to cool. Continue until all the mixture has been used.

Makes about 15 crisps

BLINIS

These little yeast pancakes make wonderful starters or pre-dinner drinks nibbles, topped with crème fraîche or thick soured cream and smoked salmon or caviar. I make a pile during the run-up to Christmas and freeze them when cold. Thaw out and warm through in the simmering oven. Of course, if you have time they are best eaten freshly made. For a more substantial starter, make the blinis larger.

225g/8oz plain flour
1 sachet of easy-blend yeast
1 tsp salt
375ml/13fl oz warm milk
1 egg, beaten
1 egg, separated

In a bowl, place the flour, yeast and salt. Using a large whisk or wooden spoon, beat in the milk, beaten egg and the egg yolk until smooth. Cover with a damp tea-towel and stand on a trivet at the back of the Aga, until risen and frothy.

Whisk the remaining egg white and then fold into the yeast batter.

Brush the simmering plate with the wire brush and, using oil on a pad of kitchen paper, oil the simmering plate lightly. Drop small spoonfuls of batter onto the simmering plate. When bubbling on the top turn them over using a fish slice. Cook for 1–2 minutes then remove. Continue cooking to use all the batter.

Serve warm or cold.

Makes about 80 cocktail blinis

PARSNIP AND GOATS' CHEESE SOUFFLÉS

These soufflés make lovely starters, but ensure that everyone is ready to eat as soon as the dishes come out of the oven because they won't stay looking impressive for long.

450g/1lb parsnips, chopped
salt & pepper
1 tbsp Parmesan cheese
225g/8oz goats' cheese
4 eggs, separated
2 tbsp chopped chives

Put the parsnips in a saucepan with a heatproof handle and add about 2.5cm/1 inch of water and a pinch of salt. Bring to the boil and drain. Cover and place in the simmering oven until the parsnips are soft enough to mash; the time will depend upon the age of the parsnips.

Lightly butter 6 individual ramekin dishes and dust them inside with the Parmesan cheese.

Mash the drained parsnips to a purée and beat in the goats' cheese, egg yolks, chives and pepper.

Whisk the egg whites until stiff but not dry. Beat 1 tablespoon of egg white into the parsnip mixture and then gently fold in the rest. Divide the mixture among the ramekins and stand on a baking tray. Put the shelf on the third set of runners from the top of the roasting oven and slide in the soufflés. Bake for 15–17 minutes, until risen and golden-brown.

Serve immediately.

Serves 6

MEATBALLS WITH TOMATO SAUCE

My family enjoy this warming, economical dish in the dreary months after Christmas. Serve with tagliatelle or creamy mashed potatoes.

1 slice of bread
2 tbsp milk
225g/8oz minced beef
225g/8oz minced pork
4 tbsp chopped parsley
2 cloves of garlic, crushed
1 egg, beaten
2 tbsp olive oil
440g/15½oz can of chopped tomatoes
1 tbsp tomato purée
sugar
4–6 tbsp red wine
1 tsp dried oregano or basil
salt & pepper

If the bread has a hard crust, remove it. Put the bread on a plate and soak in the milk. Put the meat, parsley and garlic in a bowl and mix well. I find this is best done with your hands. Squeeze the milk from the bread and break the bread into the meat mixture. Add the egg and mix thoroughly. Take a tablespoonful of the mixture and form into balls. Place on a plate. If time permits, chill the meatballs before frying.

Heat the oil in a shallow pan with a heatproof handle and fry the meatballs until evenly browned, shaking and turning them. Stir in the tomatoes, tomato purée, pinch of sugar, red wine and oregano or basil. Season with salt and pepper.

Cover the pan with a lid and when the mixture is bubbling transfer to the simmering oven for 45 minutes.

Serves 6

BEEF CASSEROLE
WITH ANCHOVIES

Anchovies with beef may sound an odd combination, but the anchovies 'melt' to give richness to the casserole. There won't be much gravy so serve the casserole with potatoes mashed with plenty of butter and milk, and maybe a little grain mustard.

3 tbsp olive oil
1kg/2lb braising steak, cut into large pieces
350g/12oz onions, sliced
1 x 50g/2oz can of anchovy fillets, drained
2 tbsp chopped parsley
2–3 sprigs of thyme

Heat the olive oil in a flameproof casserole and brown the meat well. Remove to a plate. Stir the onions into the residue in the pan. Replace the meat and add the anchovies, parsley and thyme. Mix well and cover with a tight-fitting lid. Bring to a gentle boil on the simmering plate and then transfer to the simmering oven for 3–4 hours. The meat should be very tender. Remove any thyme stalks before serving.

Serves 6

SPICED CHRISTMAS CASSEROLE

You'll find all the spiciness and fruits that are associated with Christmas in this beef and venison casserole. It can be made well in advance and frozen, but add the dried fruits after freezing and at the end of re-heating, so that they don't become overcooked and mushy.

2 tbsp vegetable oil
450g/1lb braising steak, cut into large dice
450g/1lb stewing venison, cut into large dice
225g/8oz onions, quartered
salt
1 tsp black peppercorns, crushed
2 tsp coriander seeds, crushed
1/2 tsp ground mace
1/2 tsp ground cinnamon
pinch of allspice
1 tbsp flour
300ml/1/2 pint beef stock
2 tbsp balsamic vinegar
100g/4oz pitted prunes
100g/4oz dried apricots
grated rind & juice of 1 orange
200ml/7fl oz orange juice
150ml/1/4 pint dry sherry

Heat the oil in a frying pan and brown the meat in batches, transferring each batch to a flameproof casserole as it browns. Add the onions to the pan and fry until browning. Add to the meat. Mix together the spices, flour and salt. Sprinkle over the meat mixture in the casserole. Stir well and add any pan juices. Stand the casserole on the simmering plate and pour on the stock, then the balsamic vinegar. Bring to the boil, cover with a lid, simmer for about 5 minutes and then transfer to the simmering oven for 2–3 hours.

Put the prunes, apricots and orange rind in a basin and pour over all the orange juice and the sherry, cover and leave to soak for at least 1 hour.

Remove the casserole from the oven and strain in the fruit-soaking liquid. Re-boil and return to the simmering oven for 1 hour. Stir in the soaked fruit and heat through just before serving.

Serves 8

SWISS VENISON STEW

You need to start this rich Swiss recipe at least 5 days before eating. Serve with lightly cooked vegetables.

1kg/2lb stewing venison, cut into large bite-size pieces
1 leek, sliced
1 stick of celery, quartered
2 carrots, sliced
1 bay leaf
2 black peppercorns
1 bottle of red wine
2 tbsp vegetable oil
1 tbsp flour
a few dried ceps (optional)

Place the venison in a non-metallic bowl and add the vegetables, bay leaf, peppercorns and wine. Stir well and make sure the meat is covered in the liquid. Cover and leave in a cool place for 5–10 days, stirring from time to time.

Remove the meat from the marinade and dry on kitchen paper. Strain and reserve the marinade; discard the vegetables. Heat the oil in a flameproof casserole and brown the meat. Sprinkle over the flour and add the ceps, if using. Pour over the strained marinade to barely cover the meat. Cover, bring to the boil and transfer to the simmering oven for 2–2½ hours, until tender.

Serves 4

ROAST PHEASANT WITH APPLE AND CALVADOS CREAM SAUCE

This recipe is often called Normandy Pheasant because it uses apples and Calvados. If you don't have any Calvados, add some good English cider to the sauce. Pheasant will be available fresh in the winter, but you can use frozen birds for this recipe. Choose birds that have a good plump breast and do not overcook.

75g/3oz butter
2 pheasants
4 Cox's apples, cored and sliced
6 tbsp Calvados
150ml/1/4 pint pheasant or chicken stock
300ml/1/2 pint crème fraîche
salt & pepper

Melt 50g/2oz butter in either the small roasting tin or a flameproof casserole that will just hold the pheasants. Brown the pheasants all over in the hot butter and then turn them so that they are breast-down; this helps the juices to flow into the breast meat and keep it moist. Roast in the middle of the roasting oven for 45 minutes.

About 10 minutes before serving, heat the remaining butter in a frying pan and brown the apple slices. Transfer to a serving plate and keep warm in the simmering oven. When the pheasants are cooked add them to the platter with the apples.

Place the roasting tin on the simmering plate, heat through and pour in the Calvados. Heat the Calvados and then flame it. When the flames die down add the stock and allow to bubble well until reduced. Then stir in the crème fraîche. Bubble to a glossy sauce. Season with salt and pepper. Carve the pheasant and serve with the apples and sauce.

Serves 6

POT-ROAST PORK WITH RED CABBAGE AND APPLE

Pork, red cabbage and apple go well together and this is a good way to cook an economical shoulder joint.

3 tbsp red wine vinegar
450g/1lb red cabbage, shredded
225g/8oz eating apple, cored & sliced
1 tbsp demerara sugar
salt & pepper
700g/1½lb boneless pork shoulder, rind removed

Bring a pan of water to the boil and add 1 tablespoon vinegar. Plunge in the cabbage and return to the boil. Drain the cabbage well. Place the cabbage and apple slices in a casserole and stir in the sugar, the remaining vinegar and salt and pepper.

Score the fat on the meat and season with salt and pepper. Place the meat on top of the cabbage. Cover the casserole.

Place the shelf on the bottom set of runners of the roasting oven and slide in the casserole. Cook for 1½–2 hours, until the pork is tender.

Serve the pork slices surrounded by cabbage.

Serves 6

PORK STEW WITH DUMPLINGS

Any seasonal root vegetables can be used for this hearty stew. Serve with a bright vegetable to add colour to the plate.

25g/1oz dripping or lard
2 large onions, peeled & chopped
700g/1½lb potatoes, diced
225g/8oz turnips, diced
4 sticks of celery, chopped
8 pork chops
25g/1oz seasoned flour
600ml/1 pint chicken or vegetable stock
1 bay leaf

Suet dumplings:
225g/8oz plain flour
½ tsp baking powder
salt
100g/4oz shredded suet

Melt the dripping in a frying pan and fry the onions, potatoes, turnips and celery until softening. Drain and transfer to a flame-proof casserole dish. Dip the chops in the seasoned flour and brown in the hot frying pan. Lay the chops on top of the vegetables. Add the stock to the pan and bring to the boil and pour over the meat. Add the bay leaf. Cover the casserole and bring to the boil and then transfer to the simmering oven for 1–1½ hours.

Make the suet dumplings: place all the ingredients in a mixing bowl. Mix with enough water to make a soft but manageable dough and then form into 8 dumplings.

Remove the casserole from the oven and place the dumplings on top of the gravy. Replace the lid and put the casserole on the shelf on the floor of the roasting oven for 20–30 minutes, until the dumplings have risen.

Serves 8

BRUSSELS SPROUTS
WITH CHESTNUTS

Brussels sprouts seem to be an essential part of Christmas dinner, though, of course, they are available all through the winter. Choose small, bright green sprouts that look fresh for the best flavour; these small sprouts do not need a cross to be cut in their base stalks. For the chestnuts, use either fresh ones that can be roasted in the roasting oven for a few minutes and then peeled, or vacuum-packed chestnuts which are a very good substitute if you are in a hurry.

450g/1lb Brussels sprouts
200g/7oz chestnuts
25g/1oz butter

With the smallest sprouts that you can find, trim the stalk and only enough leaf to reveal the fresh shiny inner. Cook in a pan of fast boiling, salted water for 8–10 minutes, until just tender. Drain well.

Melt some butter in a roomy frying pan and toss in the prepared chestnuts. After 2–3 minutes, add the sprouts and toss in the butter until hot. Serve immediately.

CREAMY SAVOY CABBAGE

Cabbage is an ever-present winter vegetable that deserves to be cooked well and enjoyed. If serving boiled cabbage, simply plunge finely shredded cabbage into fast-boiling water for a few minutes until it is tender, but still crisp, and then toss in a little butter and salt and pepper. This alternative method of cooking cabbage is useful to serve with roast or grilled meat, and then no gravy is needed.

2 rashers of smoked bacon, rind removed & diced
1 onion, finely diced
1 Savoy cabbage, quartered & finely shredded
300ml/1/2 pint single cream
salt & pepper

In a roomy frying pan or shallow saucepan, start cooking the bacon until the fat starts to run. Add the onion and cook until softening and just colouring. Add the cabbage, toss well in the bacon fat and then pour in the cream. Cover and cook for about 10 minutes. Check the seasoning and serve immediately.

Serves 4–6

ROAST SWEDE

Many people roast potatoes regularly but don't often roast other root vegetables. Parsnips and carrots work well, but keep an eye on them as they burn easily because of their high sugar content. The Aga roasts these wonderful winter vegetables beautifully and it is such an easy way to cook them.

1 tbsp vegetable oil
25g/1oz butter
1 large swede, cut into medium-sized cubes
salt & pepper

Put the oil and the butter in the small roasting tin and place this on the floor of the roasting oven, until the butter has melted and the oil is hot. Toss in the swede. Hang on the top set of runners of the roasting oven for 25–35 minutes, until the swede is tender and golden-brown. The cooking time will depend upon the age of the swede. Serve with roast meat or fish.

Serves 4

POTATO GRATIN WITH LEEKS

Potatoes and leeks are a perfect combination. Use a floury variety of potato, if possible. The gratin will cook well in the bottom of the roasting oven while a joint of pork or ham is roasting above, or it can be cooked for a couple of hours in the simmering oven while a casserole is cooking.

50g/2oz butter
2 leeks, sliced
salt & pepper
grated nutmeg
700g/1½lb potatoes, thinly sliced
1 tbsp chopped parsley
225ml/8fl oz hot chicken or vegetable stock
150ml/¼ pint single cream

Use a little of the butter to grease a shallow ovenproof dish.

Melt half the remaining butter in a saucepan and fry the leeks with salt, pepper and nutmeg. Cover and cook slowly for 5 minutes.

Layer the potatoes in the buttered dish with the leeks, parsley and more salt and pepper. Pour on enough hot stock to come almost to the top of the potatoes. Dot with the remaining butter. Put the oven shelf on the floor of the roasting oven and bake the gratin for about 50 minutes, until the potatoes are tender.

Pour the cream over the potatoes, shake the dish slightly and then transfer to the simmering oven for 15 minutes.

Serves 4–6

POTATO AND FETA GRATIN

I'm aware that this is breaking my own rule, but sometimes I like to serve a typical mediterranean-style dish in the depths of an English winter to remind me of summer sunshine to come. This dish fits the bill perfectly.

1.1kg/2½lb potatoes, cut into bite-size pieces
salt & pepper
225g/8oz Feta cheese, cubed
50g/2oz butter, melted
50g/2oz black olives, pitted
sprig of thyme
100ml/4fl oz white wine
100ml/4fl oz single cream

Place the potatoes in a saucepan with a heatproof handle with 2.5cm/1 inch of water and a pinch of salt. Cover and bring to the boil. Boil for 1 minute then drain the water off and put the covered pan in the simmering oven for about 20 minutes, until the potatoes are just tender. Drain well.

Butter an ovenproof dish. Mix together the potatoes, Feta cheese, butter, olives and a sprinkling of thyme leaves stripped from the stalk. Tip into the buttered dish.

Beat together the wine, cream, salt and pepper. Pour over the potato mixture. Put the oven shelf on the bottom set of runners of the roasting oven and put in the potato dish. Bake for about 30 minutes, until the potatoes are cooked and the mixture is bubbling.

Serves 6

JERUSALEM ARTICHOKES WITH CHEESE

Jerusalem artichokes are a member of the sunflower family and have nothing to do with globe artichokes. They are a knobbly root vegetable that can be cooked like parsnips, though they only require scrubbing; peeling is sometimes impossible because they are so knobbly. If you do peel Jerusalem artichokes before cooking put them in acidulated water straight away to prevent browning.

450g/1lb Jerusalem artichokes, peeled, if liked
300ml/1/2 pint milk
25g/1oz butter
25g/1oz flour
salt & pepper
grated nutmeg
100g/4oz Emmental cheese, grated

Place the Jerusalem artichokes in either a saucepan with a heatproof handle, or a flameproof casserole, with about 2.5cm/1 inch of water and a pinch of salt. Cover and bring to the boil. Drain off the water and place the covered pan in the simmering oven for about 30 minutes, until the artichokes are tender. Butter an ovenproof dish. Slice the artichokes and put in the dish.

Make a sauce by placing the butter, flour and milk into a saucepan and whisk on the simmering plate until boiling. When the sauce has thickened and is smooth, season with pepper and nutmeg. Stir in half the cheese and pour the sauce over the artichokes. Sprinkle on the remaining cheese and bake on the second set of runners from the top of the roasting oven for about 10 minutes, until bubbling and golden-brown.

Serves 4

STUMP

This strangely named vegetable dish is a useful way to use up older root vegetables to accompany meat dishes. Any combination of root vegetables can be used but do add some carrots for colour.

225g/8oz carrots, sliced
225g/8oz swede, diced
225g/8oz potatoes, diced
225g/8oz parsnips, sliced
25g/1oz butter
150ml/1/4 pint milk
salt & pepper

Place the vegetables and a pinch of salt in either a saucepan with a heatproof handle or a flameproof casserole, with 2.5cm/1 inch of water. Cover, bring to the boil on the boiling plate and boil for 1 minute. Drain off the water and place the covered pan in the simmering oven for 40–50 minutes, until the vegetables are tender.

Mash the vegetables well with the butter and the milk and adjust the seasoning. Serve hot.

Serves 4

CELERIAC WITH TOMATO SAUCE

Celeriac is an increasingly popular winter and early spring root vegetable; it tastes like celery, but has a different texture.

25g/1oz butter
1 large onion, finely chopped
2 cloves of garlic, crushed
400g/14oz chopped tomatoes
1 tbsp tomato purée
2 tbsp red wine
2 tbsp chopped parsley
1 bay leaf
salt & pepper
1kg/2lb celeriac, thickly sliced
1 tsp lemon juice
100g/4oz wholemeal breadcrumbs
50g/2oz Cheddar cheese, grated

Heat the butter in either a saucepan with a heatproof handle or a
flameproof casserole, and fry the onion until soft. Add the garlic,
cook for 1–2 minutes and then add the tomatoes, tomato purée,
wine, parsley, bay leaf and salt and pepper. Cover, bring to the boil
and place in the simmering oven for 30 minutes.

Put the celeriac in a bowl of water acidulated with the lemon juice.
Bring a pan (with a heatproof handle) of water to the boil. Drain
the celeriac and plunge into the boiling water. Return to the boil,
boil for 1 minute and drain off the water. Place the celeriac in the
simmering oven for 20 minutes, until just tender. Drain and place in
a buttered ovenproof dish. Remove the bay leaf from the sauce and
then pour the sauce over the celeriac. Mix together the breadcrumbs
and cheese and sprinkle over the sauce. Bake on the third set of runners from the top of the roasting oven for 20–30 minutes, until the
topping is golden-brown.

Serves 4

VEGETARIAN PARCEL

Every year I try to think of a fresh vegetarian idea for my Christmas cookery demonstrations. This recipe has been as popular with the meat-eaters as the vegetarians.

3 red peppers, seeded & quartered
50g/2oz butter
1 onion, finely chopped
150ml/¼ pint double cream
grated nutmeg
salt & pepper
425g/15oz ready-rolled puff pastry
225g/8oz mushrooms, sliced
450g/1lb spinach
225g/8oz Ricotta

Place the peppers, skin side uppermost, in the small roasting tin. Hang on the top set of runners of the roasting oven for 30–40 minutes. Peel if liked.

Melt 25g/1oz butter in a saucepan and fry the onion until soft but not brown. Stir in the mushrooms and cook until all the liquid has evaporated. Add the cream and allow to bubble until all the mushrooms are coated. Set aside.

Melt the remaining butter in a large pan and add the spinach. Cook with a lid on until the spinach has wilted. Toss in the butter, drain off any excess liquid and then roughly chop. Season with nutmeg, salt and pepper.

Cut the pastry in half and lay one half on a baking tray. Spread the Ricotta over the pastry, leaving a small border all round the pastry edge. Layer on the peppers and the spinach and finish with a layer of mushrooms. Season.

Roll out the remaining pastry to make it slightly larger. Brush the pastry border with beaten egg and then lay the pastry sheet on top. Seal the edges and brush all over with beaten egg. Decorate the edges.

Bake on the third set of runners from the top of the roasting oven for 15 minutes until risen and golden-brown and then move to the floor of the roasting oven for 10 minutes to crisp the base.

Serves 8

CRANBERRY PLAIT

Fresh cranberries are plentiful around Christmas. They lend colour to the festive table and a sharp flavour to dishes when so much tastes sweet and rich. Test the cranberries when they are cooked and add more sugar, if necessary, but remember that the marzipan will be sweet.

225g/8oz cranberries
50–75g/2–3oz caster sugar
375g/13oz ready-rolled puff pastry
225g/8oz marzipan, diced
1 egg, beaten, for glazing
icing sugar, for dusting

Put the cranberries in a saucepan. Add 2–3 tablespoons of water and place on the simmering plate with a lid on the pan. Cook gently for about 10 minutes, until the cranberries are tender. Stir in the sugar and taste for sweetness, adding more sugar if needed. Allow to cool.

Unroll the pastry onto a baking tray. Spread the cranberries down the centre of the pastry and dot over the marzipan. Brush the edges of pastry with beaten egg. Cut the side pieces of pastry into strips about 2.5cm/1 inch wide and at an angle of 45° to the cranberry filling. Plait the pastry over the filling by placing strips of pastry, alternating side to side, over the filling. Brush with beaten egg.

Place the shelf on the third set of runners from the top of the roasting oven and slide in the cranberry plait. Bake for 15–20 minutes, until the pastry is risen and golden-brown, and then move to the floor of the oven for 5 minutes to crisp the base.

Dust with icing sugar before serving.

Serves 6

PEAR AND MINCEMEAT TATIN

This is one of the easiest Christmas-time puddings that I know. It only really works in an Aga or Rayburn. I have made it many times at Christmas cookery demonstrations using the enamel round baking dish that is sold in Aga shops.

411g/14¹/₂oz jar of mincemeat
350g/12oz puff pastry
6 pears, peeled, cored & quartered

Line a 30cm/12 inch enamel, round baking dish with re-usable baking paper. Lay the pears in the dish to resemble the spokes of a wheel. Spoon the mincemeat carefully over the pears.

Roll out the pastry to fit the dish and lay over the pear mixture. Any excess pastry can be folded in rather than trimmed, as the top now will eventually be the underside.

Put the tatin on the floor of the roasting oven and bake for 20 minutes, until the pastry is risen and golden-brown. Remove from the oven and stand for 2–3 minutes before inverting on to a serving plate. Serve with cream, ice-cream or brandy butter.

Serves 6

POACHED PEARS

What an easy dish to prepare in the Aga. Poached pears are a good winter pudding when you feel like eating something fruity and light. Cooking time will vary slightly according to the ripeness of the pears, and remember that the fruit will not fall apart in the simmering oven so you will have to prod the pears slightly with a knife to see if they are cooked. For family meals and for quicker eating I halve or quarter the pears and cook them in a shallow pan, but for smarter occasions I leave the pears whole and remove the cores from the flower ends. Then I cook them standing upright in a smaller pan. Add a little white wine to the syrup if you like.

300ml/1/₂ pint water
2 tbsp caster sugar
2 sticks of cinnamon
6 pears, peeled & quartered

Place the water, sugar and cinnamon sticks in a saucepan, put on the simmering plate and stir whilst the sugar dissolves. Bring slowly to the boil and then slide in the prepared pears. Cover with a lid and when just boiling transfer to the simmering oven for 45–60 minutes.

Serve warm or chilled.

Serves 6

CHRISTMAS BREAD AND BUTTER PUDDING

Panettone is a popular Italian bread that is eaten at Christmas. Many years ago I was given one and found it rather dry, so half was made into trifle and the other half was used for a bread and butter pudding.

75g/3oz butter, softened
½ panettone, about 450g/1lb, sliced
600ml/1 pint milk
75g/3oz caster sugar
1 tsp vanilla essence
300ml/½ pint single cream
3 eggs, beaten
100g/4oz raisins
icing sugar, for dusting

Butter a shallow ovenproof dish; one that holds about 1.7l/3 pints. Check that the dish will fit into the large roasting tin. Butter the panettone well with the softened butter. Warm the milk and stir in the caster sugar. Remove from the heat and whisk in the vanilla essence, cream and the eggs. Pour a little of the milk mixture into the buttered dish and lay in half the slices of panettone. Scatter over the raisins and layer on the remaining panettone. Strain the egg and milk mixture over the panettone.

Stand the dish in the large roasting tin and pour hot water into the tin to come half way up the sides of the dish. Slide the tin onto the bottom set of runners of the roasting oven and bake for 10 minutes. Transfer to the simmering oven for 30–40 minutes, or until set. (A smaller but deeper dish will take more time to cook.) Dust with icing sugar.

Serves 6–8

APPLE HEARTS

This is a quick and simple pudding to make on St Valentine's Day. It is also a good way to use up left-over marzipan from Christmas. The quantity of puff pastry is only a guideline as I have used ready-rolled puff pastry and pack sizes vary. If you make your own pastry, you will need about 450g/1lb).

425g/15oz ready-rolled puff pastry
175g/6oz marzipan
6 eating apples, peeled, halved & cored
1 tbsp caster sugar
1/2 tsp ground cinnamon

Cinnamon custard:
1 tbsp caster sugar
1 tsp ground cinnamon
2 tbsp custard powder
600ml/1 pint milk

Unroll the pastry or roll out home-made to approximately a 30cm /12 inch square.

Using a template or heart-shaped cutter about 10 cm/4 inch across at its widest point, cut out 12 heart shapes. Lay the pastry hearts on a baking tray. Roll out the marzipan and cut out 12 smaller heart shapes and lay on the pastry hearts. Slice each apple half, but do not cut right through. Lay an apple half on top of the marzipan. Mix the sugar and cinnamon together and sprinkle over the apple hearts.

Bake on the third set of runners from the top of the roasting oven for 15–20 minutes, until the pastry is risen and golden-brown and the apples have softened.

Make the custard: in a jug, mix the sugar, cinnamon and custard powder together and then blend in enough milk to make a smooth paste. Pour the remaining milk into a saucepan and bring to the boil. Pour immediately onto the custard mixture, stirring well. The custard should thicken and be ready to serve, but if it hasn't thickened, return to the pan and heat for 1–2 minutes, stirring constantly.

Pour some custard onto each plate and serve with an apple heart on top.

Makes 12

SWEET PICKLED DAMSONS

Sweet pickled damsons have been a winter pudding standby for as long as I can remember. Serve a spoonful with rice pudding or custard, or sieve some to make a wonderful sauce for ice cream. The damsons keep well in a cold place, even after opening.

450g/1lb damsons
225g/8oz demerara sugar
1 tbsp vinegar

Mix the fruit and the sugar and pack into sterilised jars. Add the vinegar. Place a lid on the jar but do not screw the lids down. Stand the jars on newspaper laid on the bottom of the roasting tin. Slide the tin onto the bottom set of runners of the simmering oven and leave for 1–2 hours, until the fruit has cracked but not boiled.

Remove from the oven and seal down the lids immediately. Allow to become completely cold before storing.

Makes 700g/1½lb

MINCEMEAT CAKE

I often use mincemeat to fill baked apples and to sweeten apple pies. This cake is an everyday family fruit cake, designed to be eaten quickly.

225g/8oz self-raising flour
1 tsp ground cinnamon
175g/6oz soft margarine
175g/6oz caster sugar
3 eggs, beaten
411g/14½oz jar of mincemeat
1 tbsp soft brown sugar

Grease and base-line a deep 20cm/8 inch cake tin. Put the flour, cinnamon, margarine, caster sugar, eggs and mincemeat in a mixing bowl and beat until well mixed. If you prefer to use a food mixer or food processor, do not add the mincemeat until the end of mixing otherwise the fruit will be chopped and not as appetising.

Put the mixture into the tin and level the top. Scatter over the soft brown sugar.

For a two-oven Aga, bake either in the cake baker for 1–1½ hours or stand the tin in the roasting tin, cover loosely with foil and slide onto the bottom set of runners. Put in the cold shelf on the second set of runners from the top. Bake for 50–60 minutes, until golden-brown and shrunk from the sides of the tin and a skewer inserted into the middle comes out clean.

For a four-oven Aga, put the shelf on the second set of runners from the bottom of the baking oven, put in the cake and bake for 1–1½ hours, until the cake is golden-brown and shrunk from the sides of the tin and a skewer inserted into the middle comes out clean.

Allow to sit in the tin for about 15 minutes and then turn on to a wire rack to cool.

Serves 8

CHOCOLATE AND GINGER ROULADE

I love chocolate roulades at Christmas, but I am not a lover of chestnut purée, a traditional filling, so I decided to try a crystallised ginger filling. Serve for a special occasion.

6 eggs, separated
150g/5oz caster sugar
50g/2oz cocoa
50g/2oz crystallised ginger, chopped
1 tbsp ginger syrup
300ml/¹/₂ pint double cream, whisked
50g/2oz plain chocolate, melted
icing sugar, for dusting

Line the large tin with re-usable baking paper or baking parchment. Whisk together the egg yolks and caster sugar until thick and pale. Fold in the cocoa. Whisk the egg whites until stiff and beat 1 tablespoonful of egg white into the cocoa mixture. Then gently fold in the remaining egg whites. Pour into the tin and lightly level the surface. Hang on the bottom set of runners of the roasting oven and bake for 10 minutes, until firm to the touch. Cool slightly and then invert onto a plain sheet of re-usable baking paper or baking parchment. Leave until cold.

Fold the ginger and the syrup into the cream.

Remove the lining from the roulade and spread with the cream mixture. Roll the roulade up lengthways. Roll onto a serving plate or board. Drizzle over the melted chocolate and dust with icing sugar.

This roulade will be easier to slice if it is chilled for 1–2 hours before serving.

Serves 8–10

LIGHT CHRISTMAS CAKE

Barbara Morgan from Llanelli gave me this recipe. Barbara is a very enthusiastic cook and often comes to my cookery demonstrations at her local Aga showroom, although I doubt that there is much that I can teach her. If you have a two-oven Aga and no cake-baker, cook the cake for 30 minutes in the roasting oven with the shelf on the floor and the cold shelf on the second set of runners from the top of the oven. Then transfer to the simmering oven for 3–4 hours.

225g/8oz glacé cherries, halved
100g/4oz crystallised pineapple, chopped
50g/2oz crystallised ginger
100g/4oz candied peel, chopped
50g/2oz citron peel, chopped
225g/8oz sultanas
50g/2oz angelica, chopped
4 tbsp brandy
100g/4oz walnuts, chopped
225g/8oz butter
225g/8oz caster sugar
grated rind of 1 lemon
4 eggs, beaten
100g/4oz plain flour
100g/4oz self-raising flour
¼ tsp salt

Soak all the fruit in the brandy for 2–3 hours or overnight. Base-line and butter the sides of a deep 20 cm/8 inch cake tin. Cream together the butter and sugar until light and fluffy. Add the lemon rind. Gradually beat in the eggs, beating well between each addition. Gently fold in the flour, the soaked fruit and walnuts all at once. This way the fruit is coated with flour to stop it sinking to the bottom. Spoon the mixture into the prepared tin and level the top.

For a two-oven Aga, cook in a cake-baker for 2 hours.

For a four-oven Aga, put the oven shelf on the bottom set of runners of the baking oven and bake for 1 hour, then transfer to the simmering oven for 3–4 hours, until the cake is risen, golden-brown and a skewer inserted in the middle comes out clean. Cool in the tin.

CHOCOLATE BREAD

This chocolate loaf will appeal to young and old alike. My children like it with butter and Hugo even puts chocolate spread on as well. I like to dunk my slices in coffee. I always make this recipe for Christmas morning breakfast.

25g/1oz fresh yeast
1 tsp caster sugar
about 300ml/¹/₂ pint warm water
450g/1lb strong plain flour
25g/1oz cocoa powder
1 tsp salt
100g/4oz chocolate chips
2 tbsp soft brown sugar
1 tbsp cooking oil

Blend the yeast and caster sugar together in a basin with a little of the warm water. Stand on the Aga for 1–2 minutes, until frothing.

In a large bowl, mix together the flour, cocoa powder, salt, chocolate chips and brown sugar. Stir in the yeast, oil and most of the remaining water. Mix to a manageable but moist dough, adding all the water, if necessary. Turn onto a floured surface and knead until the dough is smooth and elastic. Return the dough to the bowl, cover with a damp tea-towel and stand on a trivet on the Aga until doubled in size.

Grease and flour 2 x 450g/1lb loaf tins. Gently knock back the dough and divide in half. Shape and fit each half into a tin. Return to the top of the Aga and cover again with the damp tea-towel and leave until risen to just above the top of the tin.

Put the oven shelf on the third set of runners from the top of the roasting oven and slide in the loaf tins. Bake for 25 minutes, until the loaves have risen and sound hollow when tapped underneath.

Turn out and cool on a wire rack.

CHRISTMAS TREE ROLLS

I brought the idea for this recipe back from America. I reduced the amount of spices but you can add more mixed spice if you like spicy buns. I find the Aga cold shelf is about the right size to make this on and you will need a large board for serving.

25g/1oz yeast
75g/3oz caster sugar
about 300ml/¹/₂ pint warm water
450g/1lb strong plain flour
salt
¹/₂ tsp mixed spice
100g/4oz glacé cherries, halved
100g/4oz sultanas
75g/3oz butter, melted
2 eggs, beaten
beaten egg, for glazing
icing sugar, for glacé icing

Blend the yeast and sugar together and mix with a little of the warm water. Stand on the Aga until frothy.

In a large bowl, mix together the flour, salt, spice and fruit. Add the yeast, melted butter and eggs. (If you are making the dough in a food processor, add the dried fruit after the first rising.) Add enough warm water to make a manageable dough. Tip onto a lightly floured work surface and knead well to make an elastic dough. Return to the bowl and cover with greased cling film. Stand on a trivet on the Aga until doubled in size.

Line the cold shelf with re-usable baking paper or grease and flour the shelf well. Knock back the dough and divide into 25 even portions. Roll each portion into a ball. Make a tree shape, starting with one ball at the top, two on the next row and three on the third row and so on until there are four balls left. Use these to make a 'pot'. Cover with greased cling film and stand on a trivet to rise until doubled in size.

Brush the dough balls with the beaten egg and slide onto the third set of runners from the top of the roasting oven for 25–35 minutes, until risen, golden-brown and hollow-sounding when tapped underneath. Cool on a wire rack. Make a little glacé icing with the icing sugar and water and drizzle in zigzags over the tree.

Makes 1 x 850g/1³⁄₄ lb loaf

BRANDY SNAP BASKETS

Brandy snaps are very easy to make. To serve as an accompaniment they can be rolled around wooden spoon handles, but I like to make baskets and fill with fresh fruits or lemon mousse. Put the filling in at the last minute so that the brandy snap doesn't have time to soften. I use cups or ramekin dishes to mould the baskets around so that they will sit on the serving plate. Make a few more than you actually need in case they break before serving.

50g/2oz plain flour
½ tsp ground ginger
50g/2oz soft brown sugar
1 generous tbsp golden syrup
50g/2oz butter, diced
finely grated rind of ½ lemon
1 tsp lemon juice

Grease the outside of 6 ramekin dishes. Line the cold shelf with a sheet of re-usable baking paper, or grease a baking tray.

Sift the plain flour and ginger onto a plate. Place the remaining ingredients in a saucepan and heat gently on the simmering plate, stirring constantly until the butter has melted and the mixture is well blended. Remove from the heat and beat in the flour mixture, until smooth.

Use a teaspoon to put 6 heaped spoonfuls of mixture, evenly spaced, onto the prepared tray. Slide the tray onto the bottom shelf of the roasting oven for 5 minutes, until golden-brown. Careful: they burn easily.

Remove from the oven and allow to firm up for 1–2 minutes before laying each brandy snap over an upturned ramekin dish. The mixture should fall in folds round the sides of the dish; if the mixture is a little firm, stroke the brandy snap down to form a basket shape. Cool before removing. Continue until all the mixture has been used up.

Makes about 10 baskets

Dried Orange Slices with Cinnamon

I make these at Christmas-time to use as decorations and add a seasonal aroma to the house. When drying the orange slices do not be alarmed if a puddle of water appears on the floor in front of the Aga. Sometimes the flue can't cope with the amount of moisture that is being driven off from the oranges.

oranges, fairly thinly sliced
cinnamon sticks
string or raffia

Put the rack inside the large roasting tin. Slice the oranges fairly thinly and lay out on the rack in a single layer. Hang the tin on the middle set of runners of the simmering oven and allow the oranges to dry out for 4–6 hours, or overnight if your Aga is not too hot.

Remove the dried orange slices from the oven and allow to cool completely. When cold, tie a cinnamon stick to each orange slice using string or raffia.

INDEX

ACKNOWLEDGMENTS

As always, thanks to my family who bear the brunt of recipe testing: to Hanna who will try anything, to Dominic who loathes mushrooms and to Hugo who tested his favourite bacon and kiwi fruit sandwich in the hope that it would fit into the book. Of course, thanks to Geoff who is so tolerant when books are 'on the go' and wades his way through mountains of washing-up. Thanks to Irene Dunn who lent me prescious books from her collection, especially the original Aga books. Thanks also to Absolute Press for commissioning this book, sensing our desire to eat more seasonally. And thanks to S & J Organics who have supplied me with weekly seasonal boxes of superb fresh vegetables, not knowing that they were the basis for much recipe testing.

Lastly, to all the Aga customers I meet at cookery demonstrations who ask for another book; my thanks.

AGA AND RAYBURN TITLES
BY LOUISE WALKER

The Traditional Aga Cookery Book (£9.99)
The Traditional Aga Party Book (£9.99)
The Traditional Aga Book of Slow Cooking (£9.99)

The Traditional Aga Box Set (£29.50)
(comprising all three of the above titles)

The Traditional Aga Book of Vegetarian Cooking (£9.99)
The Traditional Aga Book of Breads and Cakes (£9.99)
The Traditional Aga Four Seasons Cookery Book (£9.99)

The Traditional Aga Box Set 2 (£29.50)
(comprising all three of the above titles)

Traditional Aga Christmas (£14.99)

The Classic Rayburn Cookery Book (£9.99)
The Classic Rayburn Book of Slow Cooking (£9.99)

The Classic Rayburn Box Set (£19.50)
(comprising both of the above titles)

All titles are available to order from Absolute Press.

Send cheques, made payable to Absolute Press,
or VISA/Mastercard details to Absolute Press,
Scarborough House, 29 James Street West, Bath BA1 2BT.
Phone 01225 316 013 for any further details.